AGENT
INNOCENT

HOW
THE
SECRET
SERVICE
CHANGED
MY
LIFE

MELANIE LENTZ

FOREWORD BY SUE ANN BAKER

DEDICATION

For those who stayed and loved me anyway

·

TABLE OF CONTENTS

TABLE OF CONTENTS

FOREWORD

BY
SUE ANN BAKER

I N 1971, FIVE WOMEN, THEIR backs to the television and newspaper cameras, raised their hands and were sworn in as the first female agents in the US Secret Service's 106-year history. I was one of those pioneering agents. At that time, I could never have imagined the barriers that would be broken or the number of female agents who would follow in our footsteps.

Whether Melanie Lentz is in an embalming room with a former First Lady, jumping from a helicopter into the ocean, or catching pornographers, Melanie's work ethic encompasses all five points of the Secret Service's star, representing the agency's core values: duty, justice, courage, honesty, and loyalty. She started her career at twenty-two years of age as one of the youngest female agents ever hired. Her time with the Secret Service was extraordinary.

This book, however, reveals much more than what mettle it takes to be a US Secret Service agent. She writes, "I was structured, serious, and responsible, the type A perfectionist who had self-confidence issues." If you can identify with that, reading Melanie's riveting account of her journey to true adulthood will speak to you. She shares her life with a refreshing honesty and authenticity rarely revealed by a first-time memoirist.

If you are a US Secret Service buff and are always looking for glimpses into the career and life of a special agent, this detailed memoir will open the screen door to a breath of fresh air and clearly reveal what it takes to be an agent. Melanie skillfully weaves her experiences as an agent in and out of her struggles to be a good wife in a troubled marriage.

Until I read *Agent Innocent: How the Secret Service Changed My Life,* I was truly unaware of how much the duties and responsibilities of an agent have evolved. The differences between then and now are astounding. Melanie gave me a new appreciation for how far women have come within the agency. I am left with an even deeper respect and appreciation for the sacrifices *all* Secret Service agents endure. That much has not changed.

To Melanie and the women in the Secret Service, I thank you for your service. I celebrate the unique qualities and experience you all bring to the job. You carry the torch for future female agents. May that flame never go out.

— Sue Ann Baker,
Former US Secret Service Special Agent and author of
Behind the Shades: A Female Secret Service Agent's True Story

INTRODUCTION

S HE NEVER CALLED ME BY name, but she probably knew my face. Maybe she recognized my voice from our brief logistical snippets on the command post's telephone, but even that's debatable. She didn't call us often, and we only called her if there was something to relay like "Ma'am, Diane Sawyer is here for lunch."

I spent more time at her house than I did my own. That's nothing unusual for a Secret Service agent. Being away from home is part of life. It forces a flexibility you hope your families compassionately give back to you when another last-minute assignment throws a wrench in carefully laid family plans. I thought being assigned to her protection detail would allow my life to calm down a little.

Outside of work, my personal life was crumbling decidedly. No question about it, I hardly recognized who I'd become since I was hired at twenty-two. The girl standing at the Secret Service's James J. Rowley Training Center — literally shaking in her boots as she stood in formation for the first time — was brave and determined to do something meaningful with her life. She was scared because she was a very obvious outlier. But she gave

110 percent every single day regardless of the learning curve.

Fast-forward nine years and the tired and run-down woman I saw in the mirror was a complete stranger, much like the woman I was assigned to protect each day. She and I never shared a personal conversation, and I only knew what an agent needed to know to get through a workday. What's on the schedule? What time is the hairdresser coming? Is anyone else visiting today? Which nurses are working? Any threats? Any planned motorcade movements?

Logistics and protection. That's what I needed to know. My imploding personal life could wait... until it couldn't. I didn't realize then how easy it was to defuse and suppress real personal issues as trivialities because whatever I was dealing with at work was more important. Any honest Secret Service agent can relate to that at some point in his or her career. Protecting others became paramount to protecting myself.

I was angry with my "protectee" the day I had met her, but it wasn't because she'd done something wrong. I was angry because I already knew she was about to change the course of my life, and I wasn't too keen on the timing. In fact, I thought it was the worst possible timing. Hadn't I already been dealing with enough lately?

My innocence had been robbed by experience, and while my heart and intentions were still pure in their own way, I couldn't pinpoint when I had started allowing the experience to change me. I was incessantly plagued by that awful question: "Where did I go wrong?" Call me naive. Call me arrogant. Call me whatever you want. Bottom line: I never saw any of this coming until it had already arrived like an unforeseen "jackal" in a crowd at a presidential event.

When I woke up that morning, a simple phone call was the start to a really long day. I was told to meet up with my shift and drive to a predetermined location in Santa Monica, not an easy jaunt at seven a.m. from my home in the San Gabriel Valley. I hurriedly got dressed and rushed out the door.

Hours after the call, she quietly arrived via a back entrance. Other agents from the local Los Angeles Field Office were already posted around the building. She was brought into a quiet room with a lot of medical equipment, and then everyone filed out except for the two morticians tasked with her body preparations. And me. Agents would protect her until she was laid to rest, and that included what was about to happen.

As morbid as it sounds, her death was the jolt that brought me back to life, a personal defibrillator of sorts telling me not to give up. My life was just changing… a lot. And most of it wouldn't — and sometimes still doesn't — make sense.

Former First Lady Nancy Reagan's body was inside the small casket, but she was gone. Little did I know that in her death, I was about to meet her for the first time.

CHAPTER 1

THE SHY GIRL IN
THE BUSINESS SUIT

DIDN'T ALWAYS WANT TO be a Secret Service agent. It was one of those jobs I viewed as important and difficult and likely to involve rappelling from a helicopter to scoop up the president just in the nick of time. The Secret Service was definitely a team worth playing for, but picturing myself on their team, on the other hand, was a bit far-fetched (at least in my mind). I did, however, want to do something meaningful with my life. I'm painfully shy and always have been. I had never envisioned living a life in the spotlight, and I was content to make a difference from the sidelines. I just didn't know what I was "meant" to do or if that's even how it worked.

My life goals fluctuated throughout my adolescent years. I had no idea who or what I wanted to be when I grew up. But when graduate school was winding down and the reality of student loans and bills began to surface, I had to start taking the career hunt seriously. I had a bachelor's in kinesiology and was finishing a master's of science in kinesiology. Good jobs in the athletic field are competitive and hard to come by without experience or connections. I had neither.

Desperation has a way of summoning courage, and that's the only way I can describe filling out the Secret Service special agent application at twenty-one. What's the worst that could happen? They'd reject me. I had expected they would anyway. What did a shy, athletic girl fresh out of college have to offer an agency responsible for protecting America's leaders? I'd never been in a fight in my life, and I had zero military, law enforcement, or life experience. I kept a lengthy mental list of my deficiencies to keep me from getting my hopes up.

My grandpa ("Bepa") had a friend whose daughter was a Secret Service agent. Bepa was the first one to suggest that I apply. Kelli, the friend's daughter, did not have a background in law enforcement either, and she had made it through training just fine. It seemed like she was having all sorts of great adventures, or at least that's how it came across via her father over old-man conversation and coffee with Bepa. I admit, being an agent sounded exciting.

In June 2006, I printed out the agent application online after Bepa mentioned the idea to me again, probably for the hundredth time.

My college experience started as a music major in the fall of 2002. I wanted to swim in college, so I settled on California Baptist University because they had a swim team as well as a growing music program.

In my very first general education class on my very first day of college, I met Steve, a stranger initially but eventually a huge chunk of my story, like it or not. I was seventeen, and he had just turned eighteen. He sat in the back of class with his best friend Brad like the cool guys that they were. I sat somewhere in the middle with another swimmer. Many years later, I learned that when Steve saw me in class that day, he had told Brad, "If I ever have a chance with that girl, I'll marry her."

We didn't become friends right away, but I saw him almost

every day for the next four years of school. Steve was into off-roading and rock crawling, and his latest lifted rig had a bumper sticker at one point that read NO FAT CHICKS. IT WILL MAKE MY TRUCK SCRAPE. He worked part-time as a lifeguard at the pool, so it was not unusual to see him pulling off the pool covers before six a.m. as the swim team shivered in Speedos and swim caps, still rubbing our sleepy eyes and praying for a short morning practice. At home swim meets, it was guaranteed his tanned, athletic self would be perched on the lifeguard stand.

I was a walk-on with the swim team my first year, meaning I wasn't good enough for a scholarship but they let me be on the team anyway. However, where I lacked natural swimming talent, I made up for it in enviable work ethic and effort (insert pity clap). One of my coaches had referred to me as a training animal, and I had discovered I was a decent endurance athlete as opposed to the sprinter I thought I was. The coaches put me in the distance group where I stayed for the remainder of college, swimming events like the 1,650-yard freestyle ("the mile"), the 500-yard freestyle, and the 200-yard butterfly.

By the end of my freshman year, it had become apparent that being a music major and an athlete did not mix. In fact, I was the only student at the entire school who was attempting to manage both. Between the music requirements—choir rehearsals and weekend performances—and swimming obligations—practices and meets—there were too many scheduling conflicts to succeed.

I had a great freshman year in swimming and was offered a partial scholarship sophomore year. I loved music and continued to take a few courses as elective units, but I switched my major to kinesiology because, while my first love is the arts, my second is fitness. Steve, coincidentally, was also a kinesiology major, so we saw even more of each other, much to his delight and my oblivion. I knew who he was, but other than basic pleasantries and mutual friends, we weren't buddies.

If I could describe myself in college with one word, it would be *lost*. I didn't know who I was or who I wanted to be after changing my major. I'm sure most college students feel that way at some point. I doubted myself a lot, and my insecurities festered as disordered eating with intermittent bouts of compulsive exercising, severe calorie restriction, and purging. All the pretty girls only ate salad and drank Diet Coke, or so I had thought.

I'd struggled with body image and eating issues in high school, too, but not because I wasn't loved at home or because I was ever overweight. My perfectionism combined with my shyness, awkward swimmer tan lines, and consistent exposure from practically living in a bathing suit made for a true picture of insecurity. I was also lacking in the boyfriend department.

After a healthy freshman year of college, I relapsed and spent the rest of college struggling to get the purging and compulsive exercising under control. Those destructive habits would eventually catch up with me my senior year. The body is an amazing machine, but it needs maintenance or it will break down eventually.

Despite all my dysfunctions, Steve was still interested in me. He finally worked up the courage to ask me out on a date at one point during our undergraduate studies, but I was not interested and turned him down. He had gotten my number from another swimmer on my team, and I saved his number in my cell phone that day. I'm not sure why. Maybe I just wanted to know if he was ever calling me again. It wasn't that I didn't think Steve was a nice guy. He was never unkind to me, but I probably had my crush-of-the-day "bad boy" water polo player on my mind.

As my undergraduate studies came to an end in May 2006, I was still unsure of my next move. I had a consistent job teaching swimming lessons, so when I moved back to my parents' after graduation, I continued to work at the local pool until I could figure something else out. I applied to the graduate program at California Baptist University and enrolled for August 2006.

However, by that time, I'd been reading a lot about the Secret Service and had started filling out the initial application, meticulously going over my essay questions. I signed everything, had the whole packet spiral bound so it looked professional, and stuck it in my desk drawer. I was too afraid to actually submit it.

The application packet felt like it was burning a hole in my desk. I was constantly aware of its presence when I packed up my bag for work or came into my room after going for a run. I was scared that by turning it in, I'd be mocked for wanting to belong to a world I was surely unfit for. I didn't want to face the rejection. But the more I learned about the Secret Service, the more I thought about that application. I'd begun to really want the job.

Fear can be crippling, but it can also be a motivator, much like desperation. In September 2006, I realized my "college independence" time—that convenient period of adulthood without all the responsibility—was ending. That realization prompted me to drive to the Secret Service's Riverside Resident Office before one of my graduate classes to turn in my application.

Here goes nothing, I thought.

I quickly dismissed myself with the following list of why I wouldn't be hired:

1. I'm too young.
2. I have no law enforcement or military experience.
3. I have no life experience.
4. I'm too shy.
5. I've never been in a real fight. How do I expect to protect anyone?

The list went on. But in October 2006, the Los Angeles Field Office notified me that I was scheduled to take the TEA exam, the now-obsolete written test all applicants used to take, on October thirty-first.

I didn't own a business suit, but I needed one for the test. My mom took me to the Victor Valley Mall in Victorville, California, and she bought me my first business suit. She knew I was excited about even being offered the test but hesitant at expressing it. My mom is one of the kindest women I know, and she made a big deal about shopping for the suit. She was always positive I was totally capable of becoming an agent.

While we were milling about one of the department stores, a woman came up to me and asked if I was interested in modeling.

"No, not really," I said and turned back to the row of black business suits. I wasn't supermodel skinny, and I'd heard horror stories of fraudsters trying to get money from unsuspecting wannabe models at shopping malls.

"Oh, well, we were watching you shop with your mom. We think you'd be perfect for our show in a couple of weeks. We want to have some local girls walk in it."

I stared at the lady a moment to make sure she was talking to me instead of someone behind me. Didn't she see my swimmer back muscles and all the other flaws I noticed daily? But she persisted, and even my mom piped in and said, "Why not, Mel? Have some fun."

So, in a completely bizarre and out-of-character scenario, I agreed to do the show as the cashier handed over my freshly purchased black business suit and white blouse, the ensemble I would wear for every portion of the special agent application process and a suit I would keep in the back of my closet my entire career.

CHAPTER 2

A TRAINABLE APPLICANT

'M FROM THE HIGH DESERT in Southern California. It's about one hundred miles northeast of Los Angeles, and if you've ever driven from Los Angeles to Las Vegas, then you've probably passed my childhood exit while going eighty-five miles per hour. In about thirty minutes, you'd arrive at the Barstow Outlet Mall where you'd be more likely to stop for gas and In-N-Out. The nearest Secret Service Field Office was in Riverside where I went to college, about sixty miles southwest of the High Desert.

October 31, 2006, was a Tuesday. My TEA exam was scheduled for nine a.m. at the Los Angeles Field Office located in Downtown. In order for me to drive one hundred miles to the office in prime weekday traffic and make it on time, I left my parents' house in my new business suit at five a.m.

I arrived around seven thirty a.m. and waited in the parking garage. At eight a.m., I decided to head into the office building and see if there was a waiting room. When I got out of the elevator at the appropriate floor, I pushed the double doors with the US Secret Service logo on them. The office wasn't open yet, and I set off the alarm by pushing the door. It didn't open, but I looked up pathetically at the camera in the elevator landing, mortified that this was how I was starting the application process.

Someone in the office came out and disabled the alarm with a disgruntled sigh. After checking me in, I was led into the waiting room where I nervously fidgeted with my already chewed-up nails. A few minutes later, another man in a business suit was brought in. We exchanged pleasantries, and he was there to take the TEA exam too. We were the only two to take the test that day, and I never saw him again.

At nine a.m., a woman named Debbie took us to the exam room. The test was structured similarly to the SAT or ACT exams with reading comprehension and math. For some unknown and stupid reason, the TEA exam had a difficult and impractical math portion. I was always decent at math, but to my horror, Debbie gave us the five-minute warning when I was only about one-third of the way through the math questions. I quickly filled in random bubbles on the Scantron and left the test feeling dejected. Surely I had failed due to poor time management and last-minute guessing.

It's said that the squeaky wheel gets the grease, and Debbie undoubtedly viewed me as a squeaky wheel. I was told it would take about a month to get my test results sent back to me, but after two weeks, I couldn't wait any longer. I called Debbie. Maybe she could verbally tell me if I had passed.

"Melanie, you'll get your results in the mail soon," she said somewhat impatiently.

"I know. I'm so sorry to bug you. I'm just so nervous that I failed, and I'd rather just know now so I can stop getting my hopes up about this going any further."

I heard her sigh. After a moment, she said, "I don't know your score, but I know that you passed."

I tried to keep from squealing into her ear, but the way I stammered excitedly probably gave my emotions away.

"Thank you so much for telling me." I hung up the phone and went to tell my parents.

"Oh, we had no doubt you passed," my dad said.

"You always think you fail every test, and I don't think you've ever failed a test." My mom smiled and rolled her eyes at my self-doubt.

By that time, I was well into my first semester of graduate school. I was still working at a local pool nearly full time and commuting to Riverside for night courses.

A couple of weeks after calling Debbie, I got a letter in the mail saying my initial interview was scheduled for December 12, 2006, at ten a.m. It would be with the supervisor of the Riverside Resident Office. I arrived for the interview an hour early (type A perfectionist, party of one) and sat in my 1996 green Toyota Tacoma until it was an acceptable time to enter the office. I knew better than to show up too early lest I set off yet another alarm.

I stewed about the interview and mentally rehearsed my answers to potential questions like "Why do you want to be a Secret Service special agent?" As I was silently yet dramatically mouthing my answers in the car, I caught a glimpse of my reflection in the rearview mirror and stopped. I still had my nose ring in.

I went through a piercing phase in college. I liked the nose ring, but I reached up and took it out like I had also done for the TEA exam. I looked at it for a second and then tossed it into the truck's ashtray. I never put it back in again. It was time to get serious if I had any hope of becoming an agent.

The initial interview went surprisingly well. The supervisor was approachable and relatively easy to talk to. The interview was fairly informal and conversational. He said the initial interview was designed to get a general idea of what I was about, and he asked some random questions about school and my limited life experiences. Maybe he was just good at getting people to open up, but I relaxed and was a little surprised at how comfortable I felt as opposed to the usual awkwardness.

Despite my insecurities, I'd put a lot of thought into what would make me stand out other than being younger than a majority of applicants. I settled on one theme: I was trainable. I was quick to admit what I didn't know, but I advocated for my teachability and willingness to work on my weaknesses to get the job done. I had the "bones" to be a good agent, but I couldn't be expected to know everything going into it. I could be taught the skills I would need in that line of work.

After passing my initial interview, I waited for the next phase of the application process: the panel interview. In the meantime, I had finished my first semester of graduate school and had begun a new semester after the holidays. That semester brought a new graduate student along with it. Steve. He'd taken a semester off and started the same kinesiology graduate program one semester behind me.

Shortly after the new semester started, one of our mutual friends asked if we wanted to do an ultramarathon trail run in Big Bear, California, in June 2007. Big Bear City and Big Bear Lake are located about an hour from the High Desert and are popular tourist destinations as they're mountainous with a couple of ski resorts. My mom grew up in Big Bear, and we went there a lot as kids, mostly to ride our bikes around the lake or go camping. This particular race was called the Holcomb Valley Trail Run, and it was thirty-three miles of hilly trail at altitude. In other words, it wasn't a costume party 5K with a beer garden at the finish line. Our friend said she thought the two of us were the only people she knew who were crazy enough to actually do it with her. Despite Steve's disdain for running, he agreed to do it, probably because he knew I had also agreed.

But as luck would have it, our friend bailed on us with shin splints, and Steve and I found ourselves talking after class one night in early February with my day planner between us as we constructed our training plan for this beast of a run. We began to meet before classes for shorter runs, and every other weekend we drove to Big Bear for longer runs at altitude. In addition, we started going surfing and rock climbing with some mutual friends in San Onofre or Corona Del Mar beaches in Orange County, California.

Steve was always up for a fun adventure, and I genuinely enjoyed his company and positivity. It was during those training runs and surfing outings with friends that I'd realized I was developing feelings for this person who had had a crush on me since our first day of college. I looked forward to meeting at Wanda's, a café on campus, for a quick dinner after running and before class. I kept it to myself for a while even though my parents were asking about this guy named Steve who would show up at their house on weekends and drive up to Big Bear with me.

"We're just friends," I said. It was true at the time, but I think everyone could read between the lines. I had caught a case of feelings that wouldn't be going away anytime soon.

Around the time Steve and I started running together, my panel interview was scheduled at the Los Angeles Field Office. The panel consisted of one supervisor and two senior agents who would ask a series of questions, mostly scenario-based, and write a report about it. They'd decide if I should move on in the application process.

Once again, I showed up at the office in the same business suit and blouse my mom had purchased for me the previous October. When I was called into the interview room, I was instructed to take a seat opposite three stern-looking agents. In the far left chair was a male supervisor. A senior male agent sat in the middle, and a senior female agent sat on the right. After introductions, the interview began.

I wasn't sure how my panel interview went when I left the field office. Many of the questions involved law-enforcement scenarios and judgment calls for situations I'd never even remotely been exposed to. For example, I remember one particular question that went something like this.

"You and your partner are at a house to arrest a counterfeit suspect you've recently obtained a warrant for. When the front door is opened, you see four very large men sitting in the living room with your suspect. The four large men indicate that you will not be arresting their friend today. How do you respond?"

Initially I thought the appropriate response would be to go in and arrest the guy. After all, he'd broken the law. Isn't that what law enforcement is for? But when I'd paused a moment, common sense told me to take a step back. Was that really the most appropriate response? I thought it would be really reckless and stupid to die over counterfeit money. It's not like the guy was a serial killer on the loose.

I responded to the question by saying that my partner and I were outnumbered in that instance and that I would not enter the home to execute the warrant. Rather, I'd call for backup before proceeding. With no law-enforcement experience but plenty of experience watching overdramatized television, calling for backup seemed like a safe answer. None of the interviewers pressed me further on that question with a "Well, what if…?" addition to the initial scenario. They just moved on.

"You are on a protection assignment with several other agents. Management has instructed you to stay away from a particular local bar. However, you and your coworkers go to the bar anyway. One of your coworkers is caught, and when questioned by management, he says you were also there. You receive disciplinary action at work. How do you respond to your management and coworker?"

I didn't hesitate in my answer and said, "Well, I knew I shouldn't have been there in the first place, so it doesn't matter if my coworker dimed me out. I'd have to take whatever punishment was handed to me. I did something I shouldn't have done. It's as simple as that."

The supervisor looked at me as if he was surprised by my answer. It was the only time he gave anything away. "That's a really good answer," he said.

When the interview was over, I shook everyone's hands and thanked them for their time. I knew two of the three had to pass me to move forward in the application process. I knew the supervisor was probably a "yes." The other male senior agent didn't give a lot away, but I was fairly certain he was satisfied enough to push me through to the next phase. I had a feeling the female agent didn't like me, but I couldn't pinpoint anything specific that she'd said or done to make me feel that way. Maybe it was her turn to be the bad cop. I would find out later she did not want me to move on due to my age. The other two overruled her apparently.

But before I knew if I'd passed that phase in the application process, I wrote a thank-you note to the agents. I mailed it to the field office and hoped I remembered their names correctly. Thank-you notes seem old-fashioned today, but I still send them. As kids, my sister and I always wrote thank-you notes after birthday parties or holidays. My mom or dad would keep a log of who gave us which gifts so we could properly thank the giver later.

I wouldn't hear a single thing about that thank-you note until 2013. I was working the visit of Prime Minister Stephen Harper of Canada to the Los Angeles area over the Christmas and New Year holidays. The supervisor for the visit was the same supervisor in my panel. While we were waiting around for the prime minister to go to dinner, he mentioned the panel interview.

"Lentz, your panel always stood out to me because you were the only applicant I ever interviewed who sent a thank-you note."

"I figured I could use all the help I could get because I was so young."

"The note meant something, for sure, but you would have

passed the panel even if you hadn't sent it. You were young, but you weren't dumb."

After the panel interview, I waited to see if I would be moving on to the polygraph examination, the next phase of the hiring process. In the meantime, graduate courses continued, and Steve and I kept training for the trail run in Big Bear.

We had gotten to know each other pretty well during all those runs. His parents had semirecently divorced after over twenty years of marriage, and it had been a difficult transition for the family. At the time, Steve and his two brothers weren't speaking to their dad. Steve was never one to talk about his feelings at length, but he said enough to know it was a tough time for him.

I knew Steve wanted to become a police officer. He said he was working on applications at local departments and hoped to have something lined up when school was over. He knew I was in the hiring process with the Secret Service and that I had gotten my hopes up about it. Miles upon miles of running with Steve allowed for plenty of time to get to know each other, but there had been no talk of romance at that point.

In early spring 2007, I was scheduled to take a polygraph. I was instructed not to conduct any research on polygraph exams, and I was not to attempt any secret polygraph-deceiving moves during the exam. My entire education on polygraph exams came, yet again, from overdramatized television, so I was as naive about the polygraphs as I was about appropriate responses to law-enforcement scenarios.

In the Lentz household, lying was not tolerated. Ever. I remember one instance in particular when I was around twelve or thirteen years old. I was never a girly girl or obsessed with makeup, but my friends had started wearing makeup. One morning, after spending the night at my aunt and uncle's house, I woke up with a fresh pimple on my cheek or nose. I was mortified about going into public looking so hideous, so I snuck into my aunt's bathroom and dabbed some of her foundation over my blemish. I didn't know it was the wrong color for me, and I lied to my aunt when she asked if I'd been in her makeup. I never fessed up to her, so she called my mom and I got in big trouble.

My punishment was as follows: I had to use my own money to buy my aunt a new bottle of the exact foundation I had used, and I was not allowed to wear makeup or discuss wearing makeup for six months. The date was circled on the wall calendar in the kitchen.

I'm sure I cried, and I probably cried again when I apologetically handed my aunt a new bottle of her foundation. I was riddled with guilt because had I just admitted it in the first place, maybe I would have been able to ask my mom if I could cover up the pimples once in a while.

That event has always stood out to me. Looking back, it seemed so stupid to learn a valuable lesson about lying over something as simple as makeup. Maybe it was such a big deal because of how self-conscious I was about the blemishes. After all, teenagers can be so dramatic about those kinds of things. It may seem like a little lie with a harsh punishment, but to my parents, there was no such thing as a little lie.

On the day of my polygraph examination, I went in ready to tell the examiner everything about myself, leaving no details out or somehow he would know, or so I had thought.

My examiner was a large, somber agent. I was led into a dark room (at least my memory remembers it being dark and ominous) and strapped up to the machine. He asked a series of baseline questions.

"Are you Melanie Lentz?"

"Are you sitting in a chair?"

After a slew of those silly and obvious questions, he got to the important stuff.

"Have you ever worked with terrorists?"

"No."

"Have you ever used illegal drugs?"

"No."

"Have you ever broken someone's trust?"

I can liken the remainder of my polygraph to Chunk in the movie *The Goonies* when his chubby little hands were about to get shoved into a blender by the bad guys. Chunk went on a rant: "Okay, I'll tell you everything. In fourth grade…" He proceeded to admit to all his bad behavior, including making fake puke and dumping it on people at one point.

I dumped a lot on that poor guy, including an instance when I was very young and stole a doll dress from a store. My mom saw it in my hand or pocket and promptly drove straight back to the store where I had to apologize and tell the man at the counter what I had done. I distinctly remember telling my polygraph examiner about that event.

I thought my test lasted forever, and the examiner kept coming back to the drug use questions.

"You're from the High Desert. Isn't that like the meth capital of the country? You're telling me you've never tried *anything?*"

I hadn't and I maintained that I hadn't. I had never even had a sip of alcohol at that point, and I was twenty-two years old. I kept thinking, *I'm a good person. I don't do drugs, and I'm not going to become an alcoholic.* What had seemed like days of questions were really only a couple of hours. I was out of the office before lunch, convinced I'd forgotten to tell him something and I'd surely failed.

"Well, that was that," I said as I pulled out of the parking garage.

A few days later, I was notified that I'd passed the exam. Much later, I learned exams often lasted all day, and some applicants even had to return the following day to finish. Apparently my exam was on the shorter end, and agents often looked shocked when I told them about my exam.

"Your exam only lasted a couple of hours? You must be the most honest, calm person in the world. They kept me in that chair for eight hours."

The best advice one could receive about polygraph examinations was and is "Just don't lie."

Things moved quickly after the polygraph that spring. Since I'd only lived in the High Desert and Riverside, my background investigation didn't take long to complete. The investigators talked to a lot of people, including my old neighbors from Victorville. We'd since moved to Apple Valley, the next town over. I hadn't talked to some of those neighbors in years. The background investigators also talked to my professors, my coaches, my friends… everyone. I had listed references in my background packet, but they definitely didn't stop there.

The background investigators even dropped in on me at work once. I had taken a part-time job at Curves, a women's gym franchise, because they were conducting a fitness study and helping facilitate it would fulfill some of my graduate coursework requirements. I was embarrassed at how I looked when they arrived at Curves. I was dressed in hot-pink Curves workout attire with my long hair on top of my head in a messy bun, and I was jumping around being peppy and encouraging to the old ladies working out. Their wide eyes seemed to say, "Who the hell are we hiring these days? This girl is nuts."

It turned out they just needed a signature from me so they could get my tax returns. I'd already signed the authorization form, but since I'd let the finished application sit in my desk for months, the authorization had expired.

After the background investigation, I got calls from long-lost neighbors and professors saying they were so excited to hear I wanted to work for the government. Most of them confused the Secret Service and the Central Intelligence Agency, but thankfully they had good things to say about me.

"You were always a good kid, Mel. I know you're going to do great," one neighbor told me.

I was overwhelmed at the positive responses from people in

my life because I looked at myself as the painfully shy girl who could come across as rude in my shyness. I didn't expect the positivity to be so widespread.

I've said my parents led by example, and that was true in the way they treated people on a daily basis. My mom often gave away her lunch to a scrawny homeless person outside the post office or grocery store, and my dad routinely helped neighbors with car troubles or other things they couldn't afford to hire someone to fix. The kids living in the drug house across the street sometimes came over asking to use the typewriter for a school paper that had to be typed. They were always welcomed in the house, sometimes being sent home with brownies or some other goodies when they left.

The bad kids at the corner house — the teenage dudes that got into trouble a lot — sometimes drove up in their lowered trucks just to talk to my dad in the garage. My dad used to drag race, and he built roll cages for his buddy's race cars, welding and tinkering on a regular basis. Eventually he got an old 1964 GMC truck, a crew cab, and a very rare find that the bad boys loved to come admire. I'd usually fearfully run in to the house when they came by, but my dad was always welcoming to them. He showed them what he was doing and talked about cars as if they'd been friends forever. Sometimes they'd even ask my dad to fix small things on their trucks, usually because they were idiots and broke something off-roading or street racing.

When someone from the neighborhood or church was sick, my mom would cook them dinner at night so the family wouldn't go hungry with a sick loved one needing care. Those were the types of things my parents did. My parents are simply good people who wanted their children to be good people too.

I know there are some who have not seen the kindest and most respectful side of me. We all have those people in our lives. I think about them sometimes, and if given the opportunity, I have tried to right the wrongs and seek forgiveness. But despite my multitude of flaws, odd life phases, and circumstances, I'm grateful no one questioned my character when it came to my background investigation.

Once the spring semester of grad school was over in early May, I went straight into a full summer semester so I could finish the program by August in case the Secret Service wound up hiring me. Steve was still in all my classes, and we continued to train and spend more time together. Steve talked a lot about off-roading and building 4x4 off-road rigs. He had an old orange Jeep he was fabricating as a rock crawler, and he constantly had car "projects" with his buddies. He reminded me a lot of my dad who, while not into off-roading, was fascinated with how vehicles were built. Hearing him talk about building his Jeep made the miles go by quicker during our runs, and I didn't think about the altitude making my lungs sting as often.

By that point in the application process, all I had left was the physical examination and a home interview. Of all things, those two should have been easiest parts of the application process. I was athletic, so physical fitness wouldn't be an issue. But alas, there was one minor setback.

Apparently I'd had an abnormality in my EKG. The report called it a "short PR interval." I would not be allowed to move on to the home interview until being evaluated and cleared by my own cardiologist. I was devastated. I'd never had any major health issues, and I'd never seen a cardiologist in my life. I didn't even have a primary physician. How could I come this far and fail out due to some stupid PR interval?

I immediately called a local cardiologist's office and explained the situation. I made an appointment and was told a short PR interval could be a symptom of Wolff-Parkinson-White syndrome, Lown-Ganong-Levine syndrome, and possibly junctional rhythm, all conditions involving improper electrical signals in the heart.

The cardiologist was thorough, but he was not concerned. He said my PR interval was slightly shorter than normal but not so short as to cause concern. Since I was active, young, and had no history of tachycardia or other heart conditions, he told me he would provide documentation to the agency, indicating he believed I was healthy and able to be medically cleared. The agency was doing its due diligence, and that was okay, but it still gave my heart a start (no pun intended).

Finally I'd reached the last phase of the application process: the home interview. Typically, the interview took place in the presence of a spouse and children. The purpose was to give the family an idea of what the job entailed. In other words, the home interview was that moment of "real talk" when words weren't minced and the job was not portrayed as glamorous. It's when a spouse was told he or she may have to celebrate holidays alone or on an alternate day. They'd tell the family about the extensive travel, often last minute and often at inopportune times.

My home interview went a little differently. An older, retired agent named Lee came to my parents' house in late May or early June. I had baked cookies for him, but he declined. We all sat in the living room awkwardly, my sister, parents, and I sandwiched in the couch across from him.

I felt like a child who at any moment would pop up and say, "Hey, wanna come see my room?" Who was this little girl sitting on a couch with her parents saying she wanted to be a Secret Service agent?

I remember the interview going one way, but my parents recall it going quite differently. As the man got up to leave, he took my parents aside and said, "Melanie is going to do just fine." I never knew he said that until ten years later when my mom told me. I was sure I looked like a little kid at a parent-teacher conference. "Little Melanie needs to get some life experience before she tries out for any big-girl jobs, okay?" But what was going on in my head was my own skewed version of the circumstances, one point of view but not the total picture.

A few days after the interview, the phone rang at the house. Yes, we still had a landline in June 2007. It was Wayne Williams, the deputy special agent in charge of the Los Angeles Field

Office at the time.

"Melanie, we have a spot for you in Los Angeles. Do you want it?" he said simply.

"Yes!" I said without a millisecond of hesitation. This was actually happening.

I would be leaving for training in about three weeks, and my official hire date would be June 25, 2007. I hung up the phone, my hand coming to my mouth, not sure if I should cry tears of joy or fear. Was I going to be able to do this? They could picture me on their team, or they wouldn't have hired me. But could I actually earn that spot on their team?

CHAPTER 3

A PUNCH IN THE FACE

THE THREE WEEKS BEFORE MY June twenty-fifth hire date were a whirlwind. The first order of business was finishing graduate school. I would miss over a month of classes because I was leaving for the Federal Law Enforcement Training Center (FLETC) in Glynco, Georgia, on July 1. Graduate classes wouldn't let out until August. It was a lot of class to miss, and I was worried I wouldn't be able to graduate.

Since my professors in the kinesiology department had been contacted by the background investigators, they had a heads-up about what might be in my future. After speaking with them about my fate with the program, we came up with a plan that would allow me to graduate while missing some of the classes. The plan wasn't easy, and it involved presenting my final papers, research, and projects to the class earlier than anyone else. In addition, I spent the first month at FLETC training all day followed by writing papers and finishing coursework at night. But at the end of the day, I got the diploma and all was well.

On June seventeenth, Steve and I ran the Holcomb Valley Trail Run together in Big Bear. We were told we were the youngest male and female to finish it at the time. Steve's family met my family for the first time at the race. They all waited for hours while Steve and I ran a hilly thirty-three miles.

The following week after class, Steve shyly asked to talk to me as we walked to our cars. He wanted to talk about *us*. A few months prior, I had told one of our mutual friends I was falling for Steve. I knew he was interested at one point in our lives, but I was afraid that all the sweat and dirt we'd experienced together while running had made me lose my appeal. I suspect she told Steve how I felt.

I got really nervous at the word "us" and started fumbling over my words. Technically, I'd never had an official boyfriend before. I'd gone out or hung out with a few guys during college but never in an official relationship. I was scared. There were a lot of new things happening in my life.

We both leaned against our cars as we fidgeted with our keys and admitted to having feelings for each other. But I was hesitant. We both knew I was leaving until the following February. That was about eight months, and I didn't want my first real relationship to be a long-distance one. I also knew I needed to be very focused.

"I really like you, and I don't want to see anyone else. But I don't know if I'm ready to be in a relationship since I'll be gone for so long. I want to get to know you better though. I hope that makes sense." My heart was pleading for him to understand.

"I get it," he said much to my relief. "Well, why don't we keep in touch, and when you get back from training, we'll see what happens." He smiled and we awkwardly said good night. He lived near Riverside, so he got home quickly. By the time I'd merged onto the 215 freeway heading north to the High Desert, my pink Razr flip phone dinged with a text from Steve.

"I don't want to wait to call you my girl," the text read.

I smiled. Waiting seemed like the responsible and fair thing to do. But Steve didn't act intimidated or fearful of what might happen at training. Maybe I would meet someone else. Maybe I would lose interest. But he didn't say any of those things. He wanted to call me his girlfriend.

In that moment, I had a lot of respect for Steve. Up until that point, my romantic history consisted of a lot of games and guesswork, and I was sometimes the one playing the games. But Steve's directness was so refreshing. He knew what he wanted and where he wanted us to be, and he said it. I never wondered, and that made me feel desirable and cherished.

"I don't want to wait to say I'm your girl either." I smiled as I sent my reply.

And with that text, I had my first boyfriend. When I got home, it was almost midnight because class didn't let out until almost ten p.m. I turned on my desktop computer and logged into Facebook before bed. I had a new notification. Steve wanted to be "in a relationship" with me. We were going public before the clock struck midnight. How fairy tale-esque of him. I giggled like a schoolgirl, accepted the relationship, and woke up early to tell my family before they found out on social media. How cheesy it sounds today, but being social media official was enough to make my heart pitter-patter and my smile become a permanent fixture at the thought of Steve.

My parents, of course, were skeptical for the same reasons I was. They liked Steve and had gotten to know him a little when he came by on weekends for our runs. My mom made him coffee every time he came to the house, probably because she wanted him to be alert and awake as I drove the Tacoma up the windy mountain roads. Steve told me he was afraid for his life on multiple occasions because, apparently, I was not the best at navigating the windy roads.

My sister would say, "Yeah, I could have told you that was going to happen." No one, it turned out, was surprised at the news of our official relationship.

I couldn't stop smiling for the next two weeks. Steve and I spent every free moment together. I turned in my notices at both jobs, and I was frantically trying to get as much schoolwork done before leaving for training. I was also one of those annoying girls who enunciated the word *boyfriend* a little too excitedly as often as possible in conversation.

My first day as a Secret Service trainee was June 25, 2007. The first week was spent in the Los Angeles Field Office and consisted mostly of the never-ending paperwork that accompanies any government agency. My parents drove me to the airport for my flight to DC that weekend. All new agent trainees spent a week at the James J. Rowley Training Center, the Secret Service academy in Beltsville, Maryland, before starting the Criminal Investigator Training Program (CITP) in Georgia. I took a cab to my hotel where the rest of my class would also be staying.

My reporting instructions included the names of the other twenty-three trainees assigned to Special Agent Training Course (SATC) Class 273. The list included each trainee's field office assignment. I saw two additional trainees were also going to the Los Angeles Field Office and noted that there appeared to be two other females in my class.

I spent my first evening in Maryland reading and rereading my reporting instructions and ironing my clothes compulsively due to nervousness. I wanted to show up looking squared away, a phrase I'd picked up during my first week in the field office. Looking and being squared away was paramount to acceptance.

The hotel rooms had small kitchenettes and refrigerators, and the lobby had snacks and coffee available all day and night. That evening, I got on the elevator to grab a snack in the lobby. Three people joined me in the elevator, all of whom were in my class. There was Chris, a big and tall former football player and police officer. Then there was Bill, a quieter guy assigned to Las Vegas. And finally there was Lindsey, a short fireball of a lady who I found intimidating. She was also going to Los Angeles. She was vocal and assertive, two traits I lacked. Despite being a good five or six inches shorter than me, she seemed like the kind of woman who took no one's crap. She wound up being one of the best handgun shots in the class. We exchanged pleasantries as we lingered in the lobby, but I think we were all nervous, so we didn't talk about anything of substance.

The next morning, we were picked up by our class coordinators, Roger and Sally. They would be our go-to instructors throughout training and tasked with keeping us in line and on course to graduate. They were pleasant enough but not overly friendly. Roger was a tactics instructor and very passionate about it. Sally had just returned to work after having a baby, and the other instructors would talk about how she did weighted pull-ups at seven months pregnant.

"She's one tough lady," they'd say.

We were issued laptops and old-school pagers along with other gear. Much of the first week was mind-numbing lectures and paperwork reminding us of what we were getting into.

My class was an eclectic bunch. There was one other female aside from Lindsey and me, a former Marine and state trooper. I was the youngest female by a few years. Most of the class came from law enforcement or military backgrounds. There were two other guys in my class who were my age. One had briefly been a police officer, and the other had also come straight from college. There was also a handful of Secret Service Uniformed Division officers who were making the leap over to agent. Those guys were a wealth of information because they knew a lot about the agency and what was expected of us. Plus they were all just cool dudes and fun to be around.

We took a PT test during the first week to assess our current physical fitness level. Some of the agents in Los Angeles told me not to go all out on the first test because the instructors wanted to see improvement throughout training. Since I was already in shape, they said I could afford to hold back a little bit. But that wasn't in my nature, and I went all out in the push-ups, chin-ups, sit-ups and 1.5-mile run, easily surpassing the minimum standards and finishing ahead of many of the men in the run.

One day we were instructed to meet in the mat room and line up in an alphabetical formation they always referred to as "six and four" (four rows of six trainees). I had never lined up in formation before, and I just stood there hoping someone would step up and show me how to make it happen quickly. After a "too many cooks in the kitchen" moment when a handful of guys tried to show off their leadership skills, we got our act together and tried to look tough as the instructors came into the room.

"Some of you may have never experienced what it's like to be hit in the face," one instructor said. My face turned red. I'd never been punched in the face before. He must be talking about me, I thought. My inadequacies obnoxiously set up shop in my brain.

"But today"—he interrupted my pessimistic dread—"you're all going to know what it feels like."

We were instructed to put on headgear, mouthpieces, and gloves. At least I had a little protection, I thought. It wouldn't be a real punch with the padding. Roger began to pair each trainee with another classmate of similar size. Lindsey and Michelle, the other females, were about the same height and were partnered together. I, on the other hand, at five feet nine, was much taller and was partnered with Bill, the quiet guy from the elevator. One pair at a time, we were instructed to take a swing at our partners. I stood against the wall of the mat room, chewing on my mouthpiece nervously, feeling like I might throw up.

When it was our turn, we walked to the center of the room. What happened next is a blur to me now, but the fuzziness started when Bill punched me square in the face. And it wasn't a gentle love tap.

The agents in Los Angeles told me to be a good actress in the mat room while I was at training. "No one needs to get hurt," they'd said. "Just make sure you are aggressive, but don't ever go so hard that you hurt someone. Be just dramatic enough to make you and your partner look good."

But in this case, I wasn't acting.

When we were let out of the mat room for a quick break, Bill rushed over to me.

"Melanie, I'm so sorry! I've never hit a woman in my life, and I didn't want them to make me do it twice!"

I started laughing at him because his wide eyes were earnestly begging for me to understand. The poor guy clearly felt terrible.

"I had to make it count the first time. I hope you're not mad at me."

I assured him I was not angry. He would have done me no favors by going easy on me. I needed to toughen up and learn.

My classmates recalled the events later at the hotel, and some of them could barely get their words out because of their laughter. Apparently, Bill hit me hard enough to cause my long blond ponytail to fly backward along with my bobbing head in a dramatic rippling manner. They said I tried to fight back, but having never been in a fight or taken a boxing lesson, I merely flailed unsuccessfully. I laughed as they jokingly imitated me. What a sight I must've been.

I don't remember flailing back at Bill, but at least I didn't cower. As Mike Tyson once said, "Everyone has a plan till they get punched in the mouth." Mask and gloves or not, my plan to stay trainable and work hard now included learning how to throw a decent punch.

CHAPTER 4

THE BEAN SPROUT
IN GEORGIA

I FLEW TO GEORGIA FROM DC with my class at the end of the week. On July ninth, we started the Criminal Investigator Training Program at the Federal Law Enforcement Training Center, known as FLETC, pronounced *flett-see* for short. The Secret Service, Immigration and Customs Enforcement (ICE), Alcohol, Tobacco and Firearms (ATF), and many other agencies had courses at FLETC while I was there. My particular training class was half Secret Service trainees and half ICE trainees, making for a class total of forty-eight.

The campus was fairly large. We stayed in old dorm-style rooms, and I was able to get a mini fridge in my room. We ate at a cafeteria where the standing joke was that trainees needed to get in line before Customs and Border Protection (CBP), or there wouldn't be any food left. Supposedly CBP is known to be the portlier of the federal agencies. Most of the time, I didn't go to breakfast and instead got the sack lunches that were provided (two peanut-butter-and-jelly sandwiches) rather than stand in that stupid cafeteria line. I always ate dinner with classmates though.

There was even a bar on campus called the G-Bar. I didn't drink, so I stayed away from the G-Bar most of the time. It was usually full of trainees looking for a FLETC fling. It turned out that being able to play the I-have-a-boyfriend card was a blessing in disguise. The joke among the ladies was that we were all tens at FLETC even if we were threes in real life.

At FLETC, we learned basic tactics, fighting and control techniques, and we studied topics like interviewing, applicable legal statutes, shooting, handcuffing, searching, et cetera.

I hated FLETC. Since I'd grown up in a desert climate, experiencing Georgia in July was a frizzy-haired case of sweat and climate shock. If I were a wrestler trying to cut weight, I'm sure walking from the dorm to the mat room was enough to sweat a pound or two. Also, my dorm room wasn't near the other two girls in my class who were next door to one another and shared a Jack- and Jill-style bathroom. I didn't have a car there, so I couldn't leave unless someone gave me a ride. But campus wasn't really within walking distance to anything worth walking to. I spent a good majority of our off time by myself during the week unless someone with a car sent a page to the class asking if anyone wanted to go to Walmart.

I talked to Steve every moment I could. He was in the application process for police departments and still had one more semester of graduate school. He seemed to enjoy my training stories, and I loved hearing his voice and his smile because I could always tell when he was smiling by the way he talked. Even though we were physically apart, our conversations got much more personal than during all those training runs together. Due to the time difference between Georgia and California, it wasn't unusual for me to be falling asleep while talking to him. But I cherished every moment.

A typical day at FLETC consisted of classroom time and lectures (i.e. Death by PowerPoint) followed by some sort of

Physical Training (PT) workout—or two or three—outside. FLETC had a flag system set up to monitor the outdoor weather conditions. The big flag flying on campus determined our PT fate. A green flag meant outdoor PT was permitted because the humidity and heat were at safe levels. A red flag meant outdoor PT had to be limited to a short amount of time. And a black flag meant it was too hot and humid to safely exercise outdoors.

Sometimes the black flag would be flying all morning during classroom time, and when it was time for PT, the red one would be flying.

"Oh, come on!" someone would moan as we were sent to the locker rooms to change into PT attire. Speaking of PT attire, one of the funniest things I'd ever seen was a bunch of overgrown trainees wearing FLETC PT shorts. We picked up our shorts and T-shirt from a desk each day.

"Size?" they'd ask.

"Small, please," I'd respond, and then they'd plop them on the counter.

"Size?"

"XXL, please," most of my male classmates would say. Then when we lined up in formation for PT, a couple of poor guys would be tugging at their XXL booty shorts.

"Assholes gave me Daisy Dukes again," they'd say.

We swore the staff messed with the trainees and enjoyed every minute of it. I don't remember ever getting out of a PT session due to a black flag, and the PT clothes did not always come in the requested size.

Since I went into training already in pretty decent shape, the runs we did weren't a big deal to me. It was the heat that wasn't a joke. And I lacked upper body strength, a common issue among women. Statistically, we physiologically have narrower shoulders and lower muscle mass. It's not sexist to say that. Generally speaking, ladies have to try a lot harder in the strength department.

Leading up to training, my dad had installed a pull-up bar in my bedroom doorway, and I had been practicing my push-ups and chin-ups like a crazy person. I had probably watched too much TV, but I envisioned a lot of yelling and punishment in the form of running and push-ups like in the movies. Nonetheless, I still found the upper body exercises to be my weakness. I really wanted to get a perfect PT score by the end of training, and the push-ups were the only exercise keeping me from it.

I didn't have many nicknames growing up. Melanie was easily shortened to Mel. Boring. But the law-enforcement community loves nicknames. During one of our classroom sessions, we had an old geezer-esque instructor who thought political incorrectness was humorous and fedoras and cowboy hats were trendy classroom attire. We were being instructed on courtroom testimony and various aspects of the judicial system that particular day.

I inwardly groaned every time we got a new instructor. Most of them would typically start class with the same awful introductions.

"I'm [insert name and experience-laced résumé]. Let's see a show of hands. Former military?"

Half the class would raise their hands.

"Former law enforcement?"

The rest of the class, save a couple, would raise their hands. My hands conspicuously stayed down.

"And you," the instructor would ask while pointing to me. "What's your background?"

Then I would have to say I had no background except for college and grad school. Of course I didn't say it like that, but I might as well have. This one particular instructor had to continue on with the questions.

"Where are you from?"

"California, sir."

"That's what I thought. You look like you eat tofu and bean sprouts for breakfast. Is that right, Bean Sprout?"

And there it was. Bean Sprout, my new nickname. Lovely.

In addition to lectures and PT, we had firearms training at the range most days as well as mat room training where we practiced handcuffing and learned various fighting and defense techniques. The mat room training was all brand-new to me: the stand-up fighting, the ground fighting, the handcuffing, and control tactics for restraining suspects.

During some of the conditioning exercises, we punched the snot out of heavy bags. Sometimes the instructors would play Bas Rutten tapes, and we had to follow along with Bas's big voice calling out punch combos, et cetera. I can still hear Bas's "Defense!" calls, our signal to sprawl and pop back up as quickly as possible. I took those kinds of conditioning exercises seriously, especially after making a flailing fool of myself when Bill punched me. I needed to prove to myself that I could be a tough girl every bit as much as I needed to prove it to my class and instructors.

On one particular day, I felt pretty good during the drills. *Gosh darn it* (Remember, I didn't curse back then.), *I'm gonna learn how to freaking fight.* I tried not to be ultracompetitive during simple conditioning exercises, but I always told myself I had to keep up with the boys. Our main tactics instructor, whom I'll call "Crossfit" because he was, well, obsessed with CrossFit, came up behind me and said, "Lentz, you're a rock star!" Apparently, while some of the others were huffing and puffing toward the end of those sessions, I was maintaining my composure.

In hindsight, being in shape was a big advantage because I desperately needed the spare time to study the new law-enforcement material. After the rock star comment, I felt relief though. For once, I wasn't standing out because I didn't know something or wasn't a cop in a previous career. I stood out because I was doing something well.

But as egos go, they tend to get knocked down a peg when they start ballooning. Karma is the ego's evil twin sister who shows up at inopportune times. A few weeks after Crossfit's praise, we were doing ground-fighting drills. I was partnered with another trainee who was with ICE, and my hand got trapped under his large body during a roll because I hadn't positioned my hand properly as we were instructed. I heard and felt a pop. It hurt. The other trainee heard it too. He felt terrible and asked if I was okay. I said I was fine, and I hoped it was true.

I looked down at my hand, and it was starting to swell. I don't know how that escaped the watchful eyes of the instructors, but it did. Luckily, class was almost over, and we were able to go back to the dorms for the rest of the night. I iced my hand that evening, trying to relieve the pain and swelling. I didn't make a big deal out of it to my class. But I was scared. I didn't think it was broken, but something had definitely popped, and an injury would be devastating.

Late that night after plenty of ice and ibuprofen, I got down on the floor of my dorm room to attempt a push-up. As soon as I put weight on it, I face-planted onto the old lowest-bidder flooring. I tried again with the same result. I was not going home because of this stupid hand.

The next morning, I went to the little medical office on campus and took some of the athletic tape they had available for us. I didn't tell anyone in the office why I needed it, and they didn't ask. I wished they had nude-colored tape because the white was going to stand out. Thankfully, I had taken a whole semester in college on athletic taping techniques, so I fumbled through the process because I'd never taped my own hand before. I knew I was going to be asked questions, but after taping it up, I was able to crank out a couple of push-ups. I'll gut it out, I thought.

Crossfit did ask questions.

"Are you okay, Trainee Lentz?"

"Yes, sir."

"Do you need medical attention for your taped-up hand, Trainee Lentz?"

"No, sir," I insisted, but he squinted his eyes at me suspiciously. I felt the need to offer an explanation.

"I rolled on my hand incorrectly yesterday, and I'm taping it up for a little extra stability because it's sore and swollen, sir."

He raised his eyebrows skeptically.

"Please don't make me go to the medical office, sir. I can't get recycled to a later class because of this." I cringed inwardly as I waited for his response. We usually weren't supposed to speak so freely with the instructors.

But he let it go with a caution and recommendation to take care of it if it was an injury. I could see him watching me every time I had to put weight on it. I never missed or failed a single push-up for the remainder of training. I never went to the doctor, so I don't know what kind of injury I had sustained. It was obviously relatively minor in the long run. I still have a functioning hand. Let's not get too dramatic. I was too stubborn and afraid they'd send me packing if it were something remotely serious. Maybe they'd use it as an excuse to get the little girl out of the big boy's league. No such luck, guys. I was tougher than I looked.

About midway through FLETC training, Steve came to visit me for a weekend. I was beyond excited and growing increasingly homesick. He arrived on a Friday, and class seemed to drag on that day. I just wanted to be done and get to my man.

We had the best weekend together. We spent a day in Savannah, a city I'd never been to before. We explored and even went on a guided ghost tour. But the highlight of the weekend was not our kayaking and beach-going adventures. It was on random park benches. We talked for hours on those park benches. I think there were also some rocking chairs as well. We talked about what we wanted for the future and our dreams. He wanted to be a police officer, and it was looking like that was going to happen for him. He wanted a family, and so did I. We both valued the concept of family, and it just seemed like our dreams were colliding and compatible together. To me, we were better together than we were apart, and to my naive bleeding heart, that meant something. I liked envisioning us as a team.

I was already sure I loved Steve before he came to Georgia, but as I sat on the park benches, holding Steve's tanned hand and loving the sound of his laugh, I was sure I loved him.

I want to marry this guy, I thought at one point during the weekend.

Steve was the fun I was not. He was an adult who knew how to play. I was structured, serious, and responsible, the type A perfectionist who had self-confidence issues. He brought out a side of me I liked. I liked that we could have a serious conversation about the future one moment and then splash each other with our kayak oars the next. I wasn't the type to just wing it, and he made doing exactly that an adventure. Steve brought me out of my shell, and I was his biggest fan in the world. I loved how passionate he was about becoming a police officer. While I took some time warming to the idea of being a Secret Service agent, he always knew where he was going. He was even getting to know my family while I was gone and had invited my sister to go surfing with our friends a couple of times.

It was his loyalty and commitment that made my heart burst with love and respect for him. I was in love, and as we said our goodbyes when the weekend was over, I knew I wasn't going anywhere. I felt secure in the relationship and comfortable in a way I'd never felt before. I knew he wasn't going anywhere either. For the first time in my adult life, I felt really happy.

FLETC seemed to drag on for me after Steve left. I tried to squeeze in a flight home for a quick weekend, but my first flight got canceled after I'd checked in, and there were no other flights leaving until the following day. It wasn't going to work. I called Andy, the trainee who had driven me to the airport, and he came back to get me. I was bawling when he pulled up; Andy is the only person in the Secret Service who ever saw me cry.

The written tests weren't easy, but I passed them because I studied hard and took good notes. I hated the G-Bar, and I lived for the texts or pages saying a group was going to go out to dinner or get off campus for a while. Sometimes we would go to Saint Simon's Island on the weekends, and it seemed like the whole place was full of trainees escaping like we were.

I spent countless hours studying and practicing. In the most nonkinky sense, I'd practice handcuffing using my doorknobs or bedposts as pretend wrists. My classmates handcuffed with such finesse. One *click-click* and both wrists were cuffed. I seemed to be fumbling through it more than the others. Sometimes we'd practice together after class, but I knew I was usually the one who needed the practice.

My class was awesome, and if it weren't for their humor and banter, I'm sure FLETC would have been more miserable for me. They always were encouraging, but they teased me a lot, especially if they were going to say something dirty.

"Earmuff it, Bean Sprout," one of them would say when a hot girl walked by and they wanted to make a comment about her. One night we went out to dinner, and an old skinny biker dude with a long beard came up to me and said I was the most beautiful woman he'd ever seen. The guys nicknamed him Spike, and once in a while someone would wink and say, "If things don't work out with Steve, I'm sure Spike would take good care of you." I suppose many would say some of their comments were inappropriate, but I knew they were teasing me. And every single one of them was quick to become a protective big brother if anyone gave me a hard time.

We had a lot of final tests the last two weeks of FLETC. Crossfit had been hinting at something called the Burpee Mile for weeks, and it wound up being just as terrible as it sounded. Instead of jumping straight up at the end of the burpee, we jumped forward as far as possible and then dropped down into another burpee. A mile is a long way when you're doing it like that.

As we lined up at the start line, I squatted down to feel the track. The ground was really hot. After all, it still felt like summer in Georgia in September. I stood up, inhaled a deep breath, and closed my eyes.

God, uh, Bean Sprout here. If you're looking down on little me right now, it would be awesome if you could make things just a wee bit hotter and more humid in the next thirty seconds. You know, just enough for the black flag to pop up and this Burpee Mile to get canceled. Please? Are you there?

Wishful thinking. All of us looked like red-faced huffing piles of sweat when it was over.

Another looming event at FLETC was getting pepper-sprayed. I'd never been sprayed before, but I carried it when I went running in college. Once, the bottle started leaking on my hand because it was so old. I didn't realize it until I started wiping the sweat off my face and eyes. It was a less than pleasant experience for me, but that was nothing compared to actually getting sprayed.

My partner and I started the scenario by going into a tent with Crossfit. He instructed us to do a series of push-ups and jumping jacks to get our blood pumping and fatigue us a little. Then I braced myself for the spray.

"Open your eyes, Lentz."

As the sting permeated our eyes and faces, we were instructed to exit the tent and arrest a man in overalls holding a rake. We ran out of the tent, stumbling and squinting against the sting. We saw the role player in overalls. He was huge.

"Police! Drop the rake! Let me see your hands!" we yelled at the man as we approached. When we got close, I tripped over something (maybe my own two feet) and fell on the role player, knocking him over. I hadn't meant to do it that way, but it looked like I was trying to take him out at the knees. It worked and no one got hurt, thankfully.

After getting sprayed, we had a classroom block of training. The instructors poorly contained their amusement as we all filed into the room, our eyes bloodshot like we were a bunch of potheads with flushed faces. Gradually the sting wore off. What I didn't realize was that the spray got in my hair. That night, when I took a shower, the spray reactivated. I had some nice red streaks all down my chest and stomach where my wet hair rested. No one told me about all those kinds of female considerations or long hair problems. The other girls had shorter hair, but we had a good laugh about my stinging chest the next day.

On September 26, 2007, the day after my twenty-third birthday, I graduated from FLETC in a very anticlimactic ceremony. We didn't celebrate too much. We weren't agents yet.

But I did have a reason to celebrate. A small police department in San Bernardino County hired Steve. The department sent new hires through the Los Angeles Sheriff's Academy, and he was scheduled to start the following week. Coincidentally, we would both graduate on the same day in February 2008, he as a police officer and me as a special agent. So far so good, and life was looking up for us.

CHAPTER 5

COMMAND
PRESENCE

THE NEXT PHASE OF TRAINING was the Special Agent Training Course (SATC) at the James J. Rowley Training Center in Beltsville, Maryland. We typically referred to that portion of training as RTC or simply as Beltsville. SATC training was tailored to the Secret Service protective and investigative missions. We learned basic federal statutes and interviewing techniques at FLETC. At Beltsville, we received training on counterfeit currency and fraud investigations, fighting and control tactics with a protection element, threat investigations, and protection in general.

There were no dorms, cafeterias, or G-Bars at RTC. My class was housed in an extended-stay hotel about a half hour away. I loved being there because there was a grocery store, a Target, and some food options across the street, meaning I wasn't stranded on campus like FLETC. Our class got a lot closer at RTC, especially a group of six of us dubbed the Family Six because we always showed up for movie or dinner nights together. Our class had assigned vans, so we were able to get around if we didn't have a car. The vibe, at least for me, was much more positive outside of class. Also, riding to class in the vans made for hilarious conversations, usually at the expense of our instructors, who were relentlessly imitated and made fun of.

Steve started his police academy on the same day. Maryland's time difference was three hours ahead of California, so I would usually crawl into the back of a van to talk to him while we both drove to our academies in the morning. Steve had a much earlier start time than I did, so it worked out well. I was teased by the guys for being so gushy about my new boyfriend. Many of my classmates were married and had kids. They chuckled at my young love, but I didn't care.

We started RTC with another PT test to make sure we hadn't been slacking or partaking in too much FLETC cafeteria food. I had improved in all the categories, but the push-ups were still keeping me from that perfect PT score. RTC also required all trainees to take a water safety test. There was an indoor pool on site, and in order to become an agent, we couldn't sink like a brick in the water.

When my class took our water safety test, it was the first time I learned of the Secret Service Rescue Swimmer Program. The year prior, the movie *The Guardian* had come out starring Ashton Kutcher and Kevin Costner as US Coast Guard Rescue Swimmers. I loved the movie. The agents facilitating our water safety test were mostly rescue swimmers, and I made up my mind then and there that I was going to complete the course sometime in my career. The reality was that only a couple of women had ever passed, and usually only a handful of agents, male or female, actually passed each year.

The Rescue Swimmer program was designed to train agents to respond appropriately in a water-related emergency involving a protectee. They're on hand any time a protectee goes on, in, or near a water environment. It's not the US Coast Guard Rescue Swimming program (Aviation Survival Technician or A

School). The Secret Service program was abbreviated and — let's get real — less difficult than A School. Coast Guard rescue swimmers took part in our training as instructors alongside the Secret Service swimmers, but we focused on saving a protectee as opposed to saving everyone on board a sinking ship.

While we were waiting on the pool deck for the swim test, one classmate looked out the large window behind us and started trying to get our attention, nodding his head in the direction of the window. Just outside, President George W. Bush was getting ready to ride his mountain bike with several agents.

I don't think anyone in my class had ever actually seen the president in the flesh, so we all gathered around the window, staring like a pack of groupies. Bush was taking a swig from his water bottle as he straddled his mountain bike. Several agents on bikes surrounded him, and everyone seemed to be acting like that was a normal, if not regular, occurrence. It seemed so surreal to me to see the agents and the president in such a casual, dressed-down environment.

Beltsville was located in a heavily wooded area with a lot of little trails. I'm sure he was able to log plenty of miles in beautiful scenery (with the occasional burst of faint gunfire coming from the ranges nearby). After adjusting his helmet and stowing his water bottle, the group rode off as we all continued to stare out the window.

Our gawking was short-lived because the instructors caught on. They were unfazed at the events outside, undoubtedly a familiar scene to them.

"Get it out of your system," one instructor said.

"Why are you staring at him when you're supposed to be looking for the people who might want to hurt him?" said another.

"Can't see the bad guy if you're too starstruck by the person you're protecting," said yet another, egged on by his colleagues.

"Get your asses in the water."

We obeyed like good little children. Every agent needed to learn to remain focused and distraction-free. I conveniently learned that lesson on a pool deck as a trainee while I dreamed of becoming a lady rescue swimmer and watched the president go mountain biking.

Early on at RTC, one instructor with piercing blue eyes decided I was not aggressive enough during our baton practice. Agents are issued collapsible asp batons, those metal sticks that hurt like hell if you get hit with one. We would be tested on our baton skills at the end of that week or early the next. Every day he'd hound me about being more aggressive. Over and over. No matter how loud I was or what I did, apparently, I was still too tentative. Even Sally, our class coordinator, told me, "You've got to step it up, Lentz."

It was frustrating because I had no trouble during the FLETC baton test. I suspect the instructor was thinking he was going to flush out the bottom-of-the-barrel trainees early on. I could see how the girl who looked eighteen might be his first choice. In his defense, though, he probably thought being at RTC was his way of making sure the best agents wound up in the field.

I was a nervous wreck on baton test day. I was sure Piercing Eyes was going to be the person evaluating me and I'd fail no matter what. The test was a scenario-based exam where we'd have to demonstrate all the appropriate moves and techniques with efficient but not excessive aggression and control. One instructor was the Red Man, which meant he wore a giant, padded full-body suit, and he would be taking our beating while attacking us. For example, a scenario may be something as simple as walking a protectee from a fund-raising venue to a motorcade. The Red Man would be a surprise attacker, and the test would be in full swing until the instructors and evaluators were good and ready to stop the fight.

We usually tested alphabetically, which always put me somewhere in the middle with the last name Lentz. The class lined up around the edges of the mat room, the slew of scoring instructors attentively watching and taking notes on a clipboard, occasionally whispering to each other.

I watched my classmates command their scenes, thumping the Red Man with poise, asserting their strength by keeping their attacker away from the pretend president. Their moves were tactical and rehearsed as if they'd done it a million times. Many, I knew, had encountered similar situations in real life.

"Next!" It was already my turn.

My scenario was read by one of the instructors. I could see the doubt in his eyes when he looked up, his body language cocked and loaded with red pen and clipboard. His stance made my blood boil, and my self-doubt was forgotten for a moment as I inwardly sneered at him. I'll show you, I thought. He gave the signal, and the fight was on.

Until that moment, the person who exploded out of me had been invisible. She defended against the Red Man with authority and fury. Who was this person? Where had she been? Was my voice really that loud? He charged me once, so I didn't have time to use the baton, grabbing and swinging at me. I ducked and shoved him with all my might, nearly knocking him down as I advanced with the baton. Not today, Red Man.

"GET BACK!" I demanded.

The out-of-body blur of attacks, cringe-worthy thuds and commands seemed to go on forever, yet it was as if I were watching a stranger from the sidelines.

When it was over, I stood there a moment as the room began to feel real again. The whole room was eerily quiet, and I felt the stares. I glanced at my class, their mouths agape. Was that good? I saw a smirk on one face, the tiniest glimmer of a smile. I stood with my baton, a disheveled and sweaty mess, adrenaline still throbbing in my head. I wanted to throw my baton against the wall and scream at the instructors for doubting me.

But I didn't have to say anything. I simply handed off the baton and rejoined my class. Several subtle fist bumps and smiles were sent my way. "Nice job," one classmate whispered.

At the evaluations, I was simply told I'd passed. They gave me a score, but I didn't hear it. I was just relieved to pass, and I sincerely hoped I would give no one another instance to question my command presence. Lord knows, I was not quitting, flaws and all.

Secret Service agents carry the Sig Sauer P229 pistol on duty. During training, we practiced shooting almost every day. We would do basic target practice, shooting from barriers or from a vehicle, shotgun practice, and judgment shooting (scenario-based shooting where you have to make the appropriate decision between shooting and not shooting).

At the firing range, we typically shot with live ammo at targets or sheet metal silhouettes. During scenario-based judgment shooting, we'd use blanks, or bullets that don't fire but merely click when the trigger is pulled. Judgment shooting was nothing to take lightly. If we shot the wrong person or a friendly in a training environment, it wasn't a good day for a trainee. They didn't mess around with judgment shooting, and trainees could be sent home for lack of sound judgment, a liability not worth the risk.

Prior to training, I had very limited experience with a handgun. I went to the range a couple of times with my dad and grandpa to get some handgun practice before I left for FLETC, but I struggled to get the hang of a smooth trigger pull. I know it was a mental thing for me. I was not afraid of guns, I just couldn't seem to pull the trigger without jerking it just enough to send the bullet a little low and to the left of the bull's-eye.

I was barely qualifying—achieving a passing score—and definitely not at the top of my class in target practice. I allowed the instructors to fluster me because they constantly stopped me on the firing line. At FLETC, they usually didn't stop trainees during the course of fire unless they were doing really poorly. But the RTC instructors were constantly tweaking my grip and stopping me for additional instruction. I'd get frustrated because my hands weren't as big as the guys,' and every time they moved my hands on the Sig's grip, I would shoot even worse. I wanted them to leave me alone so I could figure it out without being stopped all the time.

I knew I wasn't a safety issue. My problem was never safety. But I kept trying. I passed but not as the star shooter, that's for sure. It wasn't until after training that I dramatically improved.

The even more frustrating part was I always did well in moving-and-shooting courses, which differed from point-and-shoot target practice because we had to move, take cover, shoot, et cetera. I enjoyed those courses, and I hit my targets. So why couldn't I point that stupid gun at a stationary paper target and hit what I wanted in a tight group of bullet holes at the center of the paper?

I was thrilled, however, the day they finally brought out the shotguns. I'd grown up trap shooting with my dad, and I was comfortable with a shotgun. Trap shooting involves shooting a clay disk that's flung into the air by a machine or other contraption. You only have a couple of seconds to track the clay disk and shoot it while it's flying. It's like bird hunting without the birds (and, for the record, I'm not a fan of sport hunting).

I know my dad was proud when my sister and I went shooting with him. The old farts with all the fancy gear and eyewear surrounded us like we'd need a lot of instruction only to have us kick their butts. I chuckle when I think of my little sister at the range, the shotgun almost as big as she was at the time, yelling "Pull!" to signal she was ready for the clay disk to be let loose. She demolished the disk into dust, unfazed by the massive recoil trying to throw her backward.

Dad demanded situational awareness and gun safety when his daughters handled firearms. Dad kept his guns in a large safe, and my sister and I never knew the combination. He still has that safe, and I still don't know the combination. He had an old Jeff Cooper gun safety VHS he popped into the VCR regularly. Even to this day, I can recite the safety rules from the video. Don't point a gun at anything unless you're prepared to destroy it. Treat all guns as if they're loaded. The list goes on. There was another kid's gun safety video we watched a few times. Jason Priestly was the host, and I can still hear the mantra for kids if they came across a gun: Stop. Don't Touch. Leave the area. Tell an adult.

I had a healthy respect for guns and the destruction they could cause when the handler was careless or negligent. Access control, in my parents' eyes, was something every gun owner should and could control. Gun control, obviously a controversial hot topic, meant nothing if authorized gun owners didn't take access-control precautions (i.e. a gun safe only the owner had the combination for).

My shotgun experience at training was similar to my sister's with the old dudes at the trap range. We lined up at the firing line. We would start with five slug rounds and five buckshot rounds. The buckshot was fired at shorter distances because it blasts a bunch of small metal balls when fired. It makes it easier to hit something because the buckshot spreads out as it heads where it's aimed. Therefore, you don't want to shoot buckshot at a long distance because it increases the odds of hitting someone or something unintended with a wayward buckshot pellet.

The slugs, on the other hand, are one big giant piece of lead fired when the trigger is pulled, and I definitely never want to get hit by one. The slugs are typically used at longer distances if needed.

On the first day of shotgun practice, we started with slugs. I had an older instructor standing behind me.

"Have you ever fired a 12-gauge shotgun before, ma'am?" he asked.

"Yes, sir," I said, but I didn't elaborate. I knew better than to blabber away on the firing line. He reminded me to hold the gun tightly with the stock tucked snugly into my shoulder to avoid getting knocked on my butt with the recoil. I nodded in understanding and listened to his instructions.

When the signal was given to fire, I racked the 12-gauge and quickly blasted the target with five slugs in a nice little bunch, reracking speedily after each shot. I could still hear my classmates' rounds going off when I was done. I must have finished before most of them. I wasn't trying to show off. I just shot how I normally had to shoot a shotgun at the trap range when I only had a second or two to hit the clay disk. Contrary to the pistol, the first shotgun course of fire was easy when the targets weren't moving like the clay disks. I looked back at the instructor who was staring at me wide-eyed.

"Well, you obviously know what you're doing, so keep doing it," he said.

Use-of-force training was emphasized and emphasized again at training (as it should be). Use-of-force scenarios were designed to teach us appropriate responses to various situations. Knowing when and where it would be deemed reasonable to use the various weapons at our disposal was something practiced heavily at RTC. If someone came at me with a knife, would it be reasonable to shoot that person? If that individual dropped the knife and held his or her hands up in surrender, could I still shoot them and be in the right? The terms "totality of the circumstances" and other jargon were used, meaning one must take in the entire situation as quickly and reasonably as possible and make the best split-second decision. Although if you're reasonable, you hope to God you never have to actually shoot anyone.

Piercing Eyes, ever the skeptic when it came to me but less so after the baton test, was involved with the judgment-fighting-and-shooting sections of training. One day in the mat room we were practicing scenarios with the blanks. Piercing Eyes was a role player and the bad guy. I had a partner in the scenario who took point and knocked on the door of our pretend suspect's house. Piercing Eyes opened the door and the scenario started.

A few seconds after the initial contact, Piercing Eyes pulled out a plastic knife (for training purposes) and came after my partner with it. I didn't hesitate. I pulled out the gun and confidently pulled the trigger in the direction of his head, my most visible portion of him at an angle that would avoid making my partner a second victim (although his ears would have hated me). I also noted no one else appeared to be behind Piercing Eyes, so I wouldn't get dinged for lack of situational awareness when a friendly went down too. Another instructor signaled the scenario had concluded.

"Lentz, that was a quick draw. Nicely done."

It's my lot in life to win you over, sir, I thought. Instead, I said, "Thank you, sir."

There was one female instructor who didn't like me, and I wasn't her biggest fan either, to be honest. During a surveillance training exercise, she decided to hassle me about not having my gun in my holster. Trainees, or the Rubber Gun squad as we often called ourselves, carried plastic guns around at both FLETC and RTC. They were designed to teach us to always know where our weapons were and to maintain control of them at all times. Getting caught without your pretend weapon was bad. And, even worse, if an instructor found your weapon, there was hell to pay, for sure.

At one point in training, a guy in my class forgot to get his plastic gun from his locker in the bathroom. His holster was empty, but none of the instructors noticed at first. He realized he had forgotten it, but I'm sure he hoped our next bathroom break would come before any practice with the guns in the mat room. No such luck. The poor guy pretended to draw his weapon in a scenario, pressing his index fingers together as if they were the barrel of a handgun and undoubtedly hoping for a stroke of luck. He got caught, and even the instructors had a hard time keeping a straight face as he stood there frozen with his fingers pointed like he was a child playing cops and robbers.

That particular surveillance exercise ventured into the surrounding towns, and we were told to leave our guns and pretend we had them. No need to freak out the locals.

I knew this instructor was just one of those female agents who had to let everyone know she was an instructor, the type of female law-enforcement officer with a chip on her shoulder who thought she had to constantly remind others of her authority to gain respect. Those types of women would wind up really annoying me on the job. But she was still an instructor and still had a say in my success at RTC. I was irritated with her for getting on me about something stupid because I hadn't done anything wrong. No one had his or her gun for this exercise. I was following the rules.

At least stress me out with something legitimate, lady, I thought.

A cursory glance around the group of instructors while she spoke told me all I needed to know: they were as annoyed with her as I was. I just said, "Yes, ma'am" because I knew better than to challenge her about it.

When we were released for the day, I heard another instructor call my name as everyone was gathering gear and bags. He was one of the most disgruntled instructors, but he was one of my favorites because he was real and authentic when it came to the job. He also started his career in the Los Angeles Field Office.

"Lentz, just play the game," he said simply and walked away. It was the best advice I could have been given in that moment, advice no one had given quite like that until that day. Someone would always find something wrong to stress me out about. If they couldn't find anything legitimate to criticize, they'd make it up.

"They're messing with you, Lentz. Just play the game, and you'll be fine," I told myself.

We got to fly home for a few days over the Christmas holidays, but I still had to report to the Los Angeles Field Office on the nonholiday days. Plus, with my parents' help, I found an apartment in the San Gabriel Valley, about twenty-five miles from the Downtown LA office and about twenty miles from Steve's new police department. But the highlight of the break was seeing Steve and my family. Steve and I talked every day in training, but because of our training schedules, it was usually more swapping stories and falling asleep than deep conversation. Steve was stressed at training but simultaneously seemed to be having the time of his life. I was having much more fun after class at RTC, but I was more stressed than I let on and went to see a doctor at one point because of some chronic digestive issues.

Steve wanted to take me off-roading while I was in town. On Christmas Eve, we took his brother's Jeep to Big Bear and hit the trails until the wee hours of the morning. I was scared to death the entire time, but it was probably the most fun I'd had with him aside from the Savannah trip. Steve was an excellent driver, and he could maneuver through the trails in the dead of night like it was a walk in the park. He knew the area well, and I suspected he was able to anticipate some of those tougher and sharper turns he seemed to navigate with ease.

He let me drive at one point. Well, he made me drive. I was fine sitting in the passenger seat watching him. Of course, we had driving training at FLETC and RTC. The RTC training was way more intense because we drove armored SUVs and limos through the driving courses. But navigating an old mountain road at midnight in a Jeep going way too fast for my comfort zone was a whole new kind of adrenaline rush. But I was a good sport and wound up having a great time driving (slowly) through the trails for the first time. Steve was beaming, saying things like, "That's my girl."

When I got back to my parents' house around three or four in the morning, I felt like such a rebel. I felt fun. *See, you can be spontaneous and adventurous, Mel,* I told myself. Being fun and exciting was a much-needed break from my ulcer-esque stress at RTC. But in just a few hours, everyone would be up for Christmas morning, and Bepa would be by the house with my grandma's ("Mema") famous cinnamon rolls. I lay in my bed, too happy to sleep.

I flew back to DC feeling refreshed and energized. Most of the final weeks of training involved protection-related instruction. We also were exposed to CS gas. The military guys in my class had already been exposed to it, but I hadn't. Since we were issued gas masks, we had to learn how to clear them and use them in the event of an emergency. However, the same instructor who told me to just play the game would later give a briefing and sarcastically say, "If you find yourself on your back staring at the sky, and you don't know how you got there, it's probably too late for the mask. Take a deep breath and it will be over soon." Nonetheless, most of the guys said the CS gas was way worse than the pepper spray. I disagreed. The CS gas didn't burn me in the shower after the fact.

Not only did we learn how to physically protect the president and other protectees, we also learned about investigating threats against those individuals. When it came to threat cases, we learned to weigh the threat for "potential for negative outcome." Essentially, did the person making the threat have not just motive but means and intent to carry out their intended negative outcome? I found that part of training fascinating, and I was happy to be assigned to the Protective Intelligence squad in LA years down the road. There was more to be learned, and I would find that out later.

The final week of training was very cold, icy, and snowy. But that didn't stop us from having to do our final PT test. One of my classmates said the wind chill was -19 degrees Fahrenheit when we ran. I was two push-ups short of a perfect score during the final PT test, and I was so frustrated. I had done more push-ups than needed, but four were not counted because my chest didn't touch the fist of the instructor who was lying on the ground with a fist under me. Each time I dropped into a push-up, I had to touch the fist. Some may say the cold was a factor, but I just said it was because I should have trained harder (or had a bigger set of breasts).

Lindsey and I had a little friendly competition going on with the chin-ups and the run. She beat me by one chin-up during the final test. We high-fived and went to the start line for the run. I felt like the Marshmallow Man because I wore several layers of clothes, and my teeth wouldn't stop chattering. We took off at the instructor's signal.

That 1.5-mile run was not on a track like FLETC but on a wooded road on campus. We ran out three-quarters of a mile and turned around and went back. When I made the turn, Lindsey was not far behind me, and we had that slow-motion stare down as we crossed paths. The race was on. I might have looked like a navy-blue marshmallow in my government-issue sweats, but I was not getting passed.

I graduated from the Special Agent Training Course at the James J. Rowley Training Center in Beltsville, Maryland, on February 8, 2008. I was twenty-three years old. I had more personal guests attend my graduation than anyone else in my class. We were only allotted a certain number of seats per graduate, but a couple of other trainees graciously gave up their seats when their loved ones were unable to attend. So I had a larger than typical cheering section consisting of my mom, dad, sister, a great aunt, a great uncle, and my grandparents. The memory of all of them beaming with pride reminds me how lucky I was to have that kind of support system. I knew they were smiling and clapping their big hearts out when my name was called: Special Agent Melanie Lentz.

As everyone mingled for pictures and introductions with families and classmates, a woman walked up to me. She was obviously an agent. The badge gave that much away.

"I've been to a lot of graduations since I've been here, and I have never seen someone look so relieved to be done with training," she said. I probably looked at her strangely because it seemed as though I should have known who the woman was, and I was embarrassed I didn't. She went on to say I had sighed a huge, exaggerated sigh as the ceremony concluded, the biggest she'd ever seen. I didn't realize my inner relief had been so obvious. She smiled at me and congratulated me, and I probably said, "Thank you, ma'am" with a dumb look on my face.

I learned later that she was the special agent in charge of training at the time. I probably should have known that.

But despite my overt relief, I was incredibly excited. I always thought I could have done better in the midst of any success. There was always something to criticize. But that day, I was proud. There were way too many people who didn't think I would make it. Perhaps it was some sort of sick satisfaction. I relished the opportunity to prove people wrong. That sigh was the first time I had relaxed since June 2007. The odds might have been stacked against me to some extent, but everyone loves an underdog story, right? Graduating from FLETC and RTC with dramatic sighs of relief was only the beginning.

CHAPTER 6

THE SUBTLE SHIFT

MY FIRST DAY IN THE Los Angeles Field Office was February 11, 2008. Steve began his field training that day too, and his field training would last until late June or July, depending on how well he did. Local police departments usually have a field-training program where all new officers are paired with senior training officers for a period of time until they're ready to be on their own in a squad car. The Secret Service doesn't have a field-training program, but agents are technically on probation for three years plus one hundred twenty days.

It's an understatement to say we were both nervous and stressed, but we were itching to officially start our law-enforcement careers. Neither of us wanted to screw up, and we knew we had a lot to lose by screwing up fresh out of training.

I arrived early on my first day, of course, and was promptly ushered to the Human Resources squad to complete paperwork and get my building access pass. I was also issued my first government take-home car, referred to as a g-ride.

RTC instructors joked about new agents being assigned the worst and oldest g-rides. My first g-ride was a maroon Chevy Lumina, affectionately known as Maroomina. Maroomina was a hand-me-down from another agent who, when he handed me the keys, admitted that he drove over railroad tracks on the way to work and routinely did so at a rate of speed capable of making Maroomina take a brief moment of flight. As a result, the hubcaps sometimes took flight as well, so he just kept them in the trunk.

I'm pretty sure Maroomina went straight to the junkyard when it was time for me to eventually trade up. But I was grateful for a take-home car. I'm sure none of my new neighbors suspected the twenty-three-year-old blonde in a piece-of-crap Lumina would be anything remotely resembling law enforcement.

A couple of days after reporting to the office, Andy, Lindsey and I—the three new Los Angeles agents—were sent to a small conference room in the Counterfeit squad. We hadn't been assigned to squads yet, but an office inspection was coming up. The Counterfeit squad was extremely behind in processing the counterfeit currency sent to the office from various locations like police departments or banks.

Secret Service Headquarters has an inspection division. If they arrived and the Counterfeit squad was still behind in their processing, it surely wouldn't fare well for the supervisors. After all, the squad generated many of their cases from processing and reading the associated police reports or notes from stores who received those counterfeit bills. Being behind in counterfeit processing likely meant cases would go stale and unsolved.

The three of us spent the first two months out of training going crazy in the counterfeit processing area with the smell of counterfeit permeating our nostrils all day. It smells differently from genuine currency, and it's hard to explain or describe except to say it smells dirtier. We all started to get bored, and I half wished I was back in training.

I didn't sign up for this, I thought. But, of course, as a twenty-three-year-old fresh out of the academy, I was still clueless about the mysterious agent world and had yet to realize that sometimes mundane and trivial tasks are a necessary evil.

I learned a few things very quickly in the Los Angeles Field Office. First, running the Baker to Vegas race with the office every year was guaranteed to get you in with upper management. Baker to Vegas is a relay race from Baker, California, to Las Vegas, Nevada. Federal and local law-enforcement agencies send their best and fastest runners to compete, and there are often hundreds of teams that flock to Las Vegas every year. It's a big deal to many agencies, especially the Los Angeles Sheriff's Department, which often placed at the top of the leaderboard in those years because they sent fresh, young academy graduates to spank the seasoned veteran cops of other agencies.

The race is usually in the spring, so when I started at the field office in February, tryouts were in full swing. At the time, all new agents were required to run the Hill upon arriving to the field office. That requirement doubled as a tryout for the Baker to Vegas team. The Hill is a five-mile run by the Los Angeles Police Department academy. It was just as it sounded: full of hills. Every Friday, agents would meet at the academy parking lot before work and post a time as the team captains looked on with their stopwatches and clipboards. The top twenty made the team, and a few others were selected as alternates in the event someone had to drop out before or during the actual race.

The day I ran the Hill, I met up with the other new agents. A man pulled in next to my car, got out, and started stretching. We'd assumed he was there to try out for Baker to Vegas.

"Morning," I said casually. He was shorter than me and looked like a runner in his fancy athletic attire. He looked quite serious about this stupid run.

Rather than say hello, he just gave us a curt nod and stared ahead as if we weren't there at all.

"What's his deal?" one of the other new agents whispered as we waited. I just shrugged. Whatever, I thought. He proceeded to outrun most of us, and we later learned he was the brand-new Protection Operations squad supervisor. He would have a lot of control and influence over my future protection assignments because his squad was responsible for manpower and logistics for all protection within the office. I developed a love/hate relationship with him because he was probably the least approachable supervisor I encountered in the office. But, on the other hand, he was competent and had creative and practical suggestions for the random security concerns that surfaced during protection assignments. For that, I respected him. Other than that, he was a jerk, or at least consistently came across that way.

I quickly grew tired of the incessant Baker to Vegas (or B2V) emails and updates about where everyone stood in the office rankings and what hotel everyone was going to be staying at, et cetera. While I was endlessly staring at counterfeit currency, senior agents and bosses were planning a big party after the run. It was a little annoying, but I kept my mouth shut.

A couple of weeks after the final tryout run, I got a call from one of the team captains.

"Hey, Lentz. Just wanted to let you know you made the B2V team. Congratulations. You're going to Vegas with us."

"Oh, awesome," I said slowly in confusion. "Thanks, but I wasn't planning on going. All the new agents had to run the Hill. I didn't realize running B2V was a mandatory thing if my time was fast enough."

"Well, uh, it's not mandatory, per se," he said with a hint of shock in his voice. "But if you make the team, it's a big deal. You should go. It will be a good start for your career."

I'd already figured out the politics surrounding the race because many of the B2V emails came from running-crazed upper management, and I think my typically suppressed rebelliousness surfaced briefly in that moment.

"No, thanks, dude. Maybe next year." With that, we concluded the call, and I revolted against Baker to Vegas until 2015, the only year I actually ran the race.

The next thing I learned about being an agent was the viral nature of the Secret Service rumor mill. At the end of March, after seeing nothing but counterfeit currency, I was assigned to the Bank Fraud squad. Brand-new agents often went there, mostly because it wasn't the end of the world to screw up a small check fraud case. It was considered a learning squad, and most of the cases didn't get prosecuted unless it was given to the Assistant United States Attorney's Office on a silver platter.

Bank Fraud had a few senior agents sprinkled in to teach us the ropes. We often made silly mistakes, and our interviewing techniques were not refined, especially mine. One of the other newer agents coined us the "Can't Get Right" squad.

During my first or second week in Bank Fraud, another female agent in the office called me on my government-issue Blackberry. The agency had since done away with the antiquated pagers we had in training.

"Hey, Mel. There's a rumor going around the office that you are screwing around with Ryan. I just thought you should know."

"Who?" I asked. She'd used his first name, and I was trying to remember last names because that's how agents usually addressed one another.

She gave me his full name, and I knew who she was talking about.

Of course the rumor wasn't true. I'd spoken to that agent before. He was leaving Bank Fraud for a new squad, and I was assigned his old desk. In fact, I accidentally locked myself in an office stairwell during the first week there. He's the one who'd found me, told me an easy way to remember which stairwell doors opened from the outside, and we'd had a good laugh about it. Perhaps someone had seen him teasing me in the hallway about it and assumed it was flirtatious.

That would not be the first time in my nine years as an agent that rumors about my alleged sexual escapades would sprout up. This initial rumor was my first taste of the nasty and skewed Secret Service rumor mill. Unfortunately, like a bunch of petty high schoolers, the truth gets blurry or, in this case, blatantly fabricated when it's passed around from person to person much like an old-school game of telephone.

"Are you serious?" I asked the caller. "That's one hundred percent untrue! I have a boyfriend whom I love very much, and I'm not going to screw that up. Who would say such a thing?"

"I know," she said. "I didn't think it was true, but rumors tend to surface when new girls get to the office. Maybe he started the rumor himself. I don't know."

When we'd hung up, I called Ryan and asked him if he started the rumor. He was upset but denied it.

"My life has been gossiped about enough, Lentz. I'm sorry you got dragged into it."

I was frustrated because I hadn't done anything wrong. Ryan told me he was married to an agent, and they'd gone through a bitter and rumor-filled divorce. He'd been through the wringer where the rumor mill was concerned.

From then on, I was skeptical of the Secret Service rumor mill, and over the years, I realized the female agents often bore the brunt of those skewed rumors. My personal life was always way more exciting and scandalous in the rumor mill than it actually was.

I told Steve about the rumor, and he shrugged it off.

"I'm not worried," he said. At least we had that at the time: trust.

Luckily for me, it became apparent that I was not a female agent who slept around on the job. I was madly in love with

Steve, and we were high on life with our fancy new badges and grown-up paychecks. Plus many agents would crudely advise other agents not to shit where you eat.

Life went on in the office, and I was assigned some hand-me-down bank fraud cases from agents leaving for new squads. I'd spent hours poring over subpoenaed bank documents and tried to get a sense of what needed to be done and who needed to be interviewed.

I hated bank fraud cases. Most of them involved stolen US Treasury checks, and around that time, many of them were tax return checks. Now, with the wonderful technological advancement of direct deposit, those cases aren't as prevalent. But in early 2008, they were assigned to new agents. The monetary loss was minimal, usually a few hundred dollars, and the thief typically stole the checks from mailboxes and cashed them at a shady check-cashing establishment. By the time the cases had been assigned to an agent, the check-cashing businesses didn't have any surveillance footage (if any existed at all), and the government had already issued the victims a replacement check. Most of those cases went nowhere and were closed out after "exhausting all investigative leads."

All Secret Service employees are probably familiar with the phrase "Sometimes you get the bear, and sometimes the bear gets you." Agents assigned to the field like me worked cases on normal workdays unless a protection assignment came along. For instance, if a foreign head of state was coming to Los Angeles to visit Universal Studios, agents in the field office would be given temporary protection assignments to fulfill the needs of the dignitary's visit. Another example would be if the president were traveling. Agents from the field offices would be tasked with providing personnel to serve as post standers at the venues (i.e. the agents posted at access points or near stages, press risers, et cetera). There is a convoluted travel rotation that was implemented in the offices, and agents on the ROTA knew not to plan anything big in their personal lives because it could be interrupted at any moment.

This figurative bear referred to the type of assignment or the duration. Sometimes you'd get the bear and have an awesome assignment in a desirable location (example: Hawaii with the Obamas). Other times the bear would get you, and you'd find yourself on a three-week temporary assignment with a dignitary who stayed out all night in shady areas of Hollywood and whose staff spoke little English to communicate a schedule adequately in advance.

One of my first trips as an agent was the April 2008 visit of Pope Benedict XVI to New York City. I had been assigned a midnight shift and posted at a pedestrian checkpoint outside the residence where he was staying. At first I was disappointed because I had thought I would never get to see the pope. I'm not Catholic, but how often does a pope come to the States? Not often.

At night, people gathered near the house, corralled by prestaged bike rack or security barriers, hoping to get a glimpse of the pope. Many sang hymns together. It was peaceful despite the crowds, the chilly night air subtly assisting in crowd management as we dutifully stood post throughout the night.

One night a group of about ten or twelve nuns gathered near the pope's residence for his visit. They were laughing and singing. They even started dancing joyfully, and their energy was contagious. No one expected the pope to come outside, but to everyone's delight and surprise, he did. In fact, he came outside on more than one night. He shook hands and blessed children, and so many around were crying as he made his way through the crowds, undoubtedly a security nightmare for the assigned Secret Service detail and his regular security, the Swiss Guard. NYPD officers and my fellow post standers watched the crowds, but thankfully there were no issues during those personal moments.

Toward the end of the pope's visit, one of the aides following him around gave me a little pouch with a rosary inside. The pope had blessed it for me, according to the giver. Other officers and agents posted outside were also given one. I didn't have to be Catholic to appreciate the kind gesture. I was twenty-three years old, standing just a few feet from the pope himself in the middle of the night, and I was holding a rosary he'd blessed. Regardless of religious affiliation, I got the bear on that trip.

Most of Steve's family is Catholic, and in a futile effort to win their approval and acceptance, I brought back a lot of commemorative merchandise from the pope's visit. All the items were blessed by the pope before his departure, his expression of gratitude to the security personnel. In hindsight, it was dumb to think a rosary could make up for the fact that I was Christian but not Catholic, but I was very excited about the gifts. They were appreciative, but over the years I would begin to realize it wouldn't matter what I did. I would never be seen as a member of the family, not just because I wasn't Catholic, but because that's just how they were when it came to outsiders penetrating their tight inner circle.

While I was getting my feet wet with protection travel and casework, Steve was still completing his field training. He didn't talk a lot about what happened during his training shifts. Once in a while he would have a funny story or an interesting dispatch call to talk about, but I sensed he was getting more and more stressed as time went on. The department made officers handwrite their reports during field training, and that, according to Steve, was taking him more time than they thought it should. His training officers had mixed feelings about him as well. One in particular seemed to like him and helped him a lot. Others didn't share his sentiments. As much as he tried to mask his concerns with confidence, I could tell he was worried about getting through field training.

We talked more about getting married during that time. We'd been together for almost a year, and I had thought it was becoming clear to our family and friends that we were in the relationship for the long haul. But we didn't talk about how our careers would inevitably conflict though. In all likelihood, I would probably not be able to stay in Los Angeles for my entire career, and he was a police officer in California. Moving out of state would likely result in him having to attend another law-enforcement academy. For the most part, the topic was avoided with a subconsciously naive mindset of "We'll worry about it when the time comes."

In May 2008, Steve was getting ready to start his final stage of field training at his department. His final training officer was a cocky, extremely overweight older officer who had made it abundantly clear he did not like Steve from the beginning. Finding out that officer was the one shadowing him through the final phase did nothing to calm Steve's anxieties. He'd fretted over every detail of his uniform and every piece of equipment he wore, constantly checking and adjusting until everything was just perfect.

I'd tried to encourage him and lift his spirits. I was convinced he would be fine and he'd prove the senior officer wrong. He was my Steve, the best guy on the planet in my mind.

The final phase of field training was rough from the very beginning. I could sense Steve's dejection after every shift. His department was between his mom's place and my apartment, so he would often come my way when he got off work. Sometimes I would have fun stories from my day's work, but I stopped being so eager to share them. I felt guilty for having a good day at work while he was being berated and second-guessed at every turn. I was mad at the training officer. Couldn't he see what I saw? Didn't he see this awesome, kind man who wanted to help people and do good in this world? Police departments need more officers with this mindset rather than officers who morph into jaded power-hungry robots in a uniform.

Then came that awful night in early June 2008. Steve was working a swing shift and wasn't scheduled to get off work until after one or two o'clock the next morning. Late that night, I got a text.

"I don't work for the department anymore," it read. "I'm headed to your place, and I don't want to talk about it." My heart sank. Steve had lost his dream job. What would I say? Or better yet, what was the right thing to say? Should I say anything?

I met him at the door. The look on his face was heartbreaking. I had never seen him like that. The positive, spontaneous, kind man I loved seemed so far away, his eyes blank and his shoulders slumped. He could hardly look at me. I hugged him and told him I was so sorry this was happening to him. We sat on my bed for what seemed like an eternity. He didn't say anything for a long time. Finally he stirred and looked at me.

"Mel, we can't get married until I get another job."

"Okay. I'm not going anywhere." And I didn't. I was sure it was a minor setback, a little blip in our adventure together. He wasn't meant to work for that department, but surely he was meant to be somewhere else. I just knew he'd figure it out.

Neither of us had known at the time that that night was not really an ending, a lost job, or a closed door. It was a beginning, a test, and a subtle shift in a tragic and toxic direction. It was the night everything began to change.

CHAPTER 7

THE FIRST
YEAR

BACK AT THE LOS ANGELES Field Office, things were busy because 2008 was an election year. During presidential campaigns, field agents (agents not assigned to permanent protection details like the president or vice president) are tasked with various advance assignments and leapfrog around the country with candidates, preparing (advancing) the security plan for each stop. There were motorcades to coordinate, threats to investigate, hotels and venues to secure, et cetera. A lead advance agent would oversee all that. Once a particular assignment was completed, the team of agents would usually head to another upcoming campaign stop and do the whole thing all over again.

There are a lot of moving parts in any advance and even more operating during the actual visits. In the absence of a specific campaign responsibility, I was given random post-standing assignments as needed, often traveling here and there as the Obama/Biden and the McCain/Palin campaigns picked up steam. Those assignments usually involved standing a post at a fund-raiser or outside a candidate's hotel room door. Basically, the advance agents would build a security plan, including the number of agents, Uniformed Division officers, and local law enforcement needed for the implementation of the security plan. The post standers would be there to implement it, plugging holes as we called it.

Advance work can be chaotic and involves putting out a lot of figurative fires to make everything go off without a hitch. Campaign advance work is its own animal because of the sheer quantity of stops and venues to advance. The bear gets a lot of campaign advance agents.

While I hated working fraud cases, I loved protection. I volunteered for everything and anything I could get. For example, agents would get their feet wet with a small site advance for a foreign dignitary before being assigned a hotel advance for a presidential candidate. But getting our feet wet was competitive and cutthroat. Agents would often resort to begging supervisors for assignments so they could start checking boxes and move on to more prestigious assignments. Every agent did it. But as with any office, bosses had their favorites, and some people were given protection opportunities sooner and more often than others.

My first site advance was actually not mine. I shadowed a senior agent on an airport advance for Hillary Clinton who was still in the 2008 campaign mix at the time. The first time we met up to go over the advance, I could tell she was skeptical and less than thrilled with having to walk me through a simple and routine airport advance. Clinton was not traveling commercially and would be landing at a small airport (or FBO) via a private aircraft. I know it would've gone much quicker had I not been asking a million questions. I soaked up all her knowledge like a sponge, and I think I won her over.

I was assigned several simple advances during my first year, a significant one being the visit of former president Jimmy

Carter to a Pasadena, California, radio station at Pasadena Community College. I was thankful for being in Bank Fraud during that advance. As a learning squad, my backup boss (a senior agent who helped us out and read our reports before they went to the boss) came by the radio site to do a practice supervisor walk-thru with me. The new Assistant to the Special Agent in Charge (ATSAIC) of the Protection Operations squad (the same boss from the Hill run) would be coming to my site days before the visit, and I would walk him through my security plan. He would ensure I'd done my job correctly and had a solid plan in place. Thankfully, my first site advance went well, and I gradually started getting more advance assignments. Advance work quickly became my favorite part of the job.

Steve, on the other hand, was very depressed after losing his job. I could only imagine what was going on in his head. He had wanted to be a police officer since he was a little kid. He was understandably devastated, and he sulked around for months. I probably didn't help matters by ranting about how pissed off I was that they'd let him go. I thought I was encouraging him by saying that department was full of idiots if they couldn't see what I saw. But in the back of my head, I had no idea what to say to him.

Meanwhile, it seemed like there was a new trip or a new case or a new assignment at every turn. I loved being busy, especially after being bored out of my mind processing counterfeit. In August, I'd spent a week standing post at the Democratic National Convention (DNC) in Denver, Colorado, and another week at the Republican National Convention (RNC) in Saint Paul, Minnesota.

The next month, I traveled to New York City for my first United Nations General Assembly (UNGA), which takes place every fall. I stood post at the Waldorf Astoria hotel where many foreign dignitaries were staying for UNGA. The Secret Service, State Department, and other security agencies were in full force for UNGA. Foreign heads of state from hundreds of nations were in one place. It's chaos, and many agents would try to get out of it, usually with little luck. For the next several years though, I would spend my birthday in New York City assigned to a different foreign dignitary each time.

As soon as I got back from UNGA, I did my first transportation advance in Los Angeles for Hillary Clinton, who was no longer in the running for the presidency but still had Secret Service protection as a former First Lady. As soon as that assignment was over, I flew to Philadelphia for a Flyers game. I was posted at the underground arrival area for Sarah Palin, who was slated to drop the puck at the start of the game. She wound up not staying for the whole game, and the host committee allowed the agents to watch the rest of the game from Palin's box seats. It was my first professional hockey game.

The Obama/McCain election season was nuts, to put it mildly. As Election Day drew closer, it felt like I'd spent more money on dry cleaning than groceries and more time completing travel vouchers than working on my cases. I'd been so busy with work that I hadn't noticed the stress in my personal life was also contributing to the fatigue.

Steve hadn't done much of anything to pick himself back up. I continued to try to be understanding and encouraging, but by November, I was starting to wonder when he was going to snap out of it and get back to his normal, motivated, and passionate self.

A few days before Election Day, I had gotten orders to go to Wyoming to stand post for Vice President Cheney for a few days and then to South Dakota for a few more days while Cheney hunted with some buddies. I was in South Dakota when Barack Obama was elected. It seems funny to me now. While campaign headquarters were going crazy and many were celebrating or conceding, I was in the middle of nowhere with Dick Cheney on a hunting trip.

As luck would have it, a blizzard was coming to South Dakota, and Cheney's plane barely made it out before the worst of it hit. Unfortunately, those standing post were not so lucky. A group of about six to eight of us got stranded in South Dakota for a few days. Most of us were from the Los Angeles Field Office, so we hung out in the hotel lobby together. After a few poker games, workouts, and attempts at sledding on large trash bags like idiots, we learned the airport finally reopened and we were able to fly home.

I learned so much during my first year out of training, but one of the biggest lessons came at the end of the year. In December 2008, just a couple of weeks after Obama had won the election, I'd gotten an assignment at the Obama's residence in Chicago around the holidays. The Presidential Protective Division (PPD) was beefing up the Obama protection detail, beginning the transition from presidential candidate to president-elect and, finally, to president.

My group arrived a couple of days before the president-elect. The Secret Service had rented the upstairs unit of a neighbor's garage to use as a makeshift command post and a place for agents and officers to leave their snacks, extra water, et cetera. It was also where we could take a break when it was our turn.

While we weren't standing in the snow or rain the entire time, we did have to walk through the snow to get to the next post when it was time to rotate. After the first shift, I went to buy some better boots because my hiking boots were not waterproof or a smart footwear choice for the assignment, a self-correcting error on my part. I sat on the counter of my hotel bathroom with my feet in the sink as I ran warm water over them until they regained their pinkness. But then again, I'm from California, and I always run a little on the cold side.

Due to the nature of the security plan around the house, it wasn't practical to leave during breaks to get coffee or food. Returning to the secure zone involved getting the car reswept by bomb technicians and K-9s, and the breaks weren't long enough for that. So we were limited to what we brought with us at shift change. It really wasn't a big deal. It wouldn't be the first or last time that scenario happened on a post-standing assignment. We just packed food and waters, and away we went. I didn't hear anyone complaining about it. It was just the way it was sometimes.

And then PPD (aka the Big Show) arrived. That was one of my first experiences working closely with PPD, and it put a sour taste in my mouth. The egos were palpable from the moment they arrived. When I'd walked inside the command post (CP) for a quick break, they gave me dirty looks, something I found odd because most of them weren't supervisors. The others standing post on my shift received the same looks. After the first day, we were told we could not use the CP anymore and would need to take our breaks elsewhere because "there just wasn't room" for PPD and those standing post. For the rest of the assignment (several more days), our breaks were taken in a minivan parked outside the CP. We were allowed to use the restroom, but then we had to leave. Since we were working in a residential area, there was nowhere else for us to go.

I knew my place as a new agent. Like any government agency, there was some hierarchy in the agent food chain. I didn't have authority issues, and I didn't have a problem saying "yes, sir" and "yes, ma'am" like the best of them. Luckily, my shift found humor in the situation by relentlessly making fun of PPD from the van. We joked that we should get sandwiches with extra raw onions and accidentally leave them in the command post fridge for a couple of days. That stench would help them maintain their sour faces. We didn't actually do anything, of course, but there was a sick satisfaction in imitating the jerks on the warm side of that assignment.

After the Chicago trip, I knew exactly what kind of agent I did not want to be. I would see many of those PPD agents again over the years, and many of them would get promoted while I was still on the job. The bear might have gotten me a little when I couldn't feel my toes in Chicago, but I learned less about my poor cold tolerance and more about being a decent person to junior agents. No one was going to say I treated junior agents poorly. I couldn't always control the assignment, but I could control how I acted and behaved no matter where the figurative bear fit into the equation.

I will admit to not being one hundred percent successful in my attitude about a bad bear from time to time, but I would reference Chicago 2008 many times in my career. Sometimes the biggest jerks teach the best lessons.

Right before the Chicago trip, the ATSAIC of Bank Fraud called me, and I found out the leave I'd requested for the end of the year was being canceled due to the visit of the Malaysian delegation to Los Angeles over the Christmas holiday.

I rang in the New Year with a lot of fun stories and experiences, but I failed to recognize that I was changing. I began swearing a lot more, which was very unlike me, and I was starting to get frustrated with Steve's fluctuating states of defeatist pessimism and lazy optimism ("It will work out somehow."). In 2008, I only took one day of accumulated vacation time (my mom's birthday) and zero days of accumulated sick leave, even though there were days I was sick and still went to work. I did have some weekends off, but by the end of the year, even those regular days off were less common.

I was getting tired but not necessarily physically tired. I was straining emotionally too, and it seemed like Steve was just playing with his buddies and off-road rigs all the time. The habits and trends of 2008 ultimately became a way of life. Like a bit of rust on an off-road rig can spread like a cancer, I failed to recognize the speck of rust in my relationship with Steve that would be ignored as it slowly spread: resentment.

CHAPTER 8

DOGS, PROPOSALS, AND COUNTERFEIT

STEVE AND I NEVER HAD a traditional dating relationship. We didn't go out on dates to get to know each other. We conveniently had school, mutual friends, and a race to train for at the beginning of our relationship. The define-the-relationship talk happened early. He didn't show up at my apartment with flowers. We didn't go to nice restaurants. And that was fine. I was never a high-maintenance kind of girl who expected jewelry or flashy romantic gestures.

I sometimes wished for a little more romance though. When I'd see some of the guys at work walk to the Farmers' Market in Downtown LA on Thursdays and come back with the five-dollar bouquets for their significant others, I'd feel a little envious or jealous. I wished for more of those little sweet gestures once in a while. But that was not Steve's style. What he did do was include me in his life. I was welcomed into the camping, off-roading, rock-climbing adventures, and I went as often as work allowed.

I was comfortable with Steve despite the lack of traditional romance, and I felt secure in our relationship even though the first two years felt like a long-distance relationship when all the training and travel added up.

I would tell people that Steve saved me from myself in a way. Once we had started training for the Big Bear race, my purging and disordered eating patterns seemed to disappear or become less of a daily factor in my life. I still struggled with self-esteem, but I wasn't acting out on them in destructive ways like I had before.

It's stupid to think that a guy could cure those deep issues, but I was convinced that he did. At FLETC and RTC, I wasn't purging either. It's almost like I had grown out of the problem. I'd also decided that I wanted to start swimming again because I really wanted to be selected for the Rescue Swimmer course. I knew I couldn't pass that course if I was unhealthy like my senior year of college. Even though I was frustrated at the way Steve was handling his unemployment setback, it never crossed my mind to walk away from the relationship.

After spending Christmas with the Malaysians, my work slowed down for a little bit. Obama's inauguration came and went, and I was able to focus on some casework and start swimming more consistently.

In February 2009, I responded to a Craigslist ad for puppies. In hindsight, buying a dog from Craigslist probably did not make me the brightest bulb in the tanning bed, but when I saw a little one-pound fur ball in a shoebox, I fell in love. I grew up with big dogs, and my family was partial to Labradors. We always had a dog (or two or three). Little Bella grew into nine pounds of spunky mixed-breed Chihuahua who had Steve wrapped around her little finger. The guy who didn't like small dogs never denied her a belly rub or a french fry.

The Bank Fraud squad was still anticlimactic, and after repeated declinations from the Assistant United States Attorney's Office when I'd present those little cases, I thought I might be wasting my time. The casework wasn't producing anything meaningful. It wasn't helping anyone or anything. It was just a task to do in between protection assignments.

So, when the Counterfeit squad asked for assistance in a big counterfeit case, I was all too happy to volunteer for surveillance. The surveillance made its way to Las Vegas in the spring of 2009 when the suspects started passing the counterfeit in the casinos.

I was assigned the morning shift, and it was usually relatively quiet except for the fact that I was constantly stopped by casino security and asked for identification.

"Excuse me, miss. How old are you?"

"Twenty-four," I would reply. He or she would ask for identification, and I would hand the security officer my driver's license. Then I would try to get the attention of another agent in the area to take over my position because I knew what was coming next.

"Ma'am, I'm going to need you to come to the security desk and get a wristband so we know you're old enough to be in here."

After the first couple of days, I just started my shift at that desk so they'd leave me alone. My colleagues, however, found it hilarious.

"Hey, little girl. You don't belong here. Where's your mommy?" I usually retorted with something like, "Nice khaki shorts. You're such a trendsetter." We'd all laugh and continue working. I was the only female on my shift, and I was a good sport about it.

I did not take that back-and-forth banter as sexual harassment. Over the years, there were instances that could be classified as such, and I definitely didn't appreciate the comments, but most of the time it was just good old-fashioned teasing. Being an agent meant you should be mature enough to take a joke. I found humor and laughter to be a good way to pass the time during long surveillances and long shifts. Plus it was nice to help with a case that was actually progressing somewhere productive, unlike the ones I was assigned in Bank Fraud.

In the meantime, Steve applied to a couple of police departments, but for one reason or another, he wasn't hired. A lot of departments were on hiring freezes, and the ones that were hiring often had hundreds of applicants for only a handful of positions. Not passing field training the first time was an easy way to disqualify him among hundreds of other qualified candidates.

Since many of my coworkers had met Steve at random barbeques or gatherings, they'd sometimes ask about him and how the job search was going. I'd always say something like, "Oh, it's competitive out there right now, but he's trying really hard."

After he hadn't been working for almost a year, a couple of people in the office started saying, "Did your boyfriend get a job yet?" every time I saw them in the office. I always (always) defended him and spoke highly of him even though some coworkers were getting bold enough to say I should see the huge red flag right in front of my face. I continued to say it was just a big setback, but it would all work out. I knew Steve better than they did, and the Steve I knew would figure something out.

But I had started to worry. He'd obviously been different since he'd lost his job—growing more distant it seemed—and I was trying to figure out if the new version was the real Steve or if the version I fell in love with was still hiding somewhere.

Once in a while, I got a glimpse of the 2007 Steve. We were getting gas one day, and he went inside to pay while I waited in his truck. After a couple of minutes, a middle-aged man walked out of the station and came up to my window.

"Are you with that guy?" he asked, nodding his head in Steve's direction. He looked tired, his hands and face weathered and dry.

"Yeah," I said.

"Well, I am in that beat-up truck over there. I'm out of gas. I was just trying to scrape enough together to get me home, and he just bought me a whole tank of gas. You've got a good one, lady."

"I know. He's a keeper," I said with a smile and wished him a good rest of the day.

Steve came back to the car with one of those awful energy drinks he had to have, and we drove off. He never said a word to me about what he'd done inside. Eventually I told him what the man said. He just shrugged it off.

"Sometimes people just need a little help," he said and cracked open his energy drink.

But by summer, talking about his job situation started turning into arguments rather than discussions. We'd had arguments before, but the frequency seemed to be increasing. My inquiries about his efforts with applications were turning into pleas and frustration. It seemed like maybe he didn't care about being a police officer anymore. I remember saying at one point, "Steve, I don't care if you're a police officer. I'll love you no matter what you decide to do. But sometimes you have to be willing to do something else in the meantime. The cop thing clearly isn't working out right now. That's okay. But you can't keep sitting around waiting for your dream job to fall into your lap."

His family and friends had also started making comments about me, implying that I did not want to hang out with them or participate in their adventures and activities anymore. "What's her problem?" they had asked Steve. It was true that I wasn't able to go off-roading or rock climbing as often. But it was never because I didn't want to. I got frustrated with Steve when he told me what they'd said because it didn't seem like he was defending me to his family and friends. Didn't they know I had a very demanding job, and I just didn't have the flexibility in my schedule like they did as students or police officers with more convenient days off? Wasn't he supposed to have my back? On top of everything, I felt like I needed to defend myself to his family and friends, and I resented Steve and them for alienating me because I was being the grown-up I had to be.

In the meantime, after trying out for the 2009 Rescue Swimmer course, I was not selected. But I kept swimming. I wasn't giving up on that dream.

In May 2009, Second Lady Jill Biden came to Los Angeles for a handful of events. Mrs. Biden's staff had told us she wanted to go running by the beach in the morning. She'd also asked that the run be as low-key as possible. She was not the first protectee to desire some privacy, but security-wise it had taken some finagling to make it happen (if we could at all). The Protection Operations squad called me and asked me to go running with her.

"Lentz, you're about as inconspicuous as any agent in the office."

They told me how far she wanted to run and what her average pace was, and I drove to Santa Monica and started scouting out routes, drop-off and pickup spots, emergency egress areas, the best places for the motorcade to shadow us, et cetera.

I loved advance work. I loved developing the security plans. I loved getting creative to make things work. I was happy during protection. I wished I could just work protection assignments and forego the investigations altogether.

I met Mrs. Biden and her motorcade at the designated drop-off spot. I borrowed a bellyband holster (a holster that straps around the stomach and is easier to conceal) and wore a large T-shirt over it so I could conceal my gun, radio, and other gear. Another agent in the office named Edward, who we called Smooth-Talking Eddie because he had a Southern accent and the best manners on the telephone, was also asked to run with us. He was young and looked more like a member of a boy band than a Secret Service agent.

Mrs. Biden was polite and wore a white running outfit. I told her what direction we were going, and she turned on her music after putting on her headphones. I ran in front and Eddie behind. Neither Eddie nor I had ever worn a bellyband while running before, and it was a little awkward. I regularly glanced back to make sure I wasn't going too slow or too fast. No one on the beach seemed to recognize Mrs. Biden.

However, no one was more surprised than I to look back and see Smooth-Talking Eddie's face beet red as he was stuffing his gun back into his bellyband. His gun had bounced out of the holster as we ran. I didn't think anyone saw it happen. Mrs. Biden was oblivious to the young new agent running a few yards behind her, flailing in horror as his issued weapon escaped its pouch during a run on the boardwalk.

I know many agents on permanent protection details think running with the vice president's wife was no big deal and a regular occurrence for them. But for me, being able to use my strengths as an athlete and my younger-looking appearance to allow a public figure to have a quiet hour of running made me feel like I had something to offer. I could plug a hole or fill a need others could not. Being a bit of a misfit had its advantages. As I've said before, I wanted more than anything to live a meaningful life. I really wanted to matter… to feel needed.

Steve worked as a substitute teacher briefly, but he hated it so much he stopped answering the calls for sub jobs. He worked briefly at a warehouse with his brother, but it was a temporary position.

Eventually he was able to get on as a reserve officer in the San Gabriel Valley city where I lived. It was an unpaid position, but it allowed him to keep his POST (Police Officer Standards and Training) certification active within the state. If he were not working as an officer for a certain period of time, he'd have to go through the academy again. Steve seemed to perk up after he started working as an officer again. He told me stories about his shifts, and that smile and passion I had missed seemed to creep back into his demeanor. But he was only working one or two shifts per week, and his savings was starting to get thin.

At one point, I, once again, suggested to Steve that maybe it was time to consider another occupation while he was getting some experience as a reserve officer. I have never been a materialistic person, and I never cared about being rich. My suggestion was not because I wanted him to give up on his dream of being a cop or because I wanted his money. I wanted to get married, and I wanted us to go back to the solid, happy, and employed couple we used to be.

I knew I couldn't support both of us because he had six-figure student loan debt. I was also a realist; sometimes life has setbacks and you have to do what was necessary to get back on your feet even if it's not what you really wanted in the long-term. I was frustrated with him. But my well-intentioned support was not delivered in a way that Steve found helpful, and as long as we didn't talk about his job search, we got along great. If I brought it up, it would result in an argument.

Late that summer, I decided it was time to get out of the apartment. Once I had a couple of pay raises under my belt with the Secret Service, I was able to afford to rent a little two-bedroom house just down the road from my apartment complex. I got permission to install a doggie door for Bella. In early fall, Steve got a Norwegian Lundehund puppy, a rare breed that looks like a little fox and has six toes on each foot. He named her Anja, and she was just beautiful. I would grow very attached to Anja and her to me. It was one of those special bonds that only dog lovers can understand.

After I had moved into the house, Steve started staying over at my place more often than his mom's. Essentially we were living together but not really telling anyone. Of course, his mom and family knew because he wasn't there, and they told him it wasn't proper for us to be living together before we were married. I didn't tell my parents because they would have had the same opinion. They weren't stupid, and I'm sure they suspected. But I didn't care at the time.

In the midst of puppy buying and home renting, I was assigned sporadic advance assignments but nothing too exciting. I was getting more experience and getting more confident and proficient in my protection work. I still asked a million questions and painstakingly went over my security plans and diagrams and paperwork.

Obama came into town a few times that year, and despite working many presidential events, I had yet to physically see him. I was usually standing at an access point well away from any of his movements within the venue. But when he attended an event at the Beverly Hilton Hotel, I was posted backstage on the opposite side of where the president would be entering and exiting. After his remarks were completed on stage, I heard the usual radio chatter alerting the motorcade of an imminent departure. As soon as he left, I would be done for the evening and able to head home.

"Um, did I go the wrong way?" a familiar voice said behind me. I turned to see none other than the president of the United States standing in front of me. I know my eyeballs widened, and I stammered like an idiot trying to find my words. Instead of saying, "Yes, sir. Right this way, Mr. President" and directing him to the correct exit, I merely pointed and said, "That way." He looked where I pointed just as the current Special Agent in Charge of the Presidential Protective Division (PPD) Joseph Clancy was rushing toward his wayward protectee. Years later, Clancy would come out of retirement for a brief stint as Director of the Secret Service. As soon as they walked off toward the motorcade, I felt pretty stupid. But after that, when people asked if I'd met the president, I could say I had… kind of.

In late October 2009, I transferred out of Bank Fraud and into the Electronic Crimes Task Force (ECTF), a multiagency task force with the Los Angeles Police Department, Los Angeles District Attorney Investigators, California Highway Patrol, Los Angeles County Sheriffs, the Federal Bureau of Investigation, and probably another agency or two sprinkled in. I had put ECTF at the top of my squad preferences because my good friend Adisa and a couple of other friends were in the squad. I was not a tech-savvy genius, but I could be taught the ins and outs. A lot of the ECTF cases were connected to fraud cases anyway because so much of banking was now electronic.

On November 21, 2009, I asked Steve if we could take a picture of the dogs and us for a Christmas card. He agreed with a slight eye roll, and we set the camera on a timer in the backyard. The moment before the shutter clicked, a ring popped up in front of my face, and that moment was memorialized forever in that year's Christmas card photo. I looked at Steve once the shutter clicked, completely shocked. I had no idea he had a ring.

He got down on one knee and told me he wanted to spend the rest of his life with me and asked me to marry him. He used words like soul mate, a concept I didn't believe in but found sweet in the moment. I was cynical and thought that if soul mates existed, I wasn't guaranteed to wind up with that person. With the divorce rate being what it is, there was a good chance my soul mate married someone else. But my heart swelled as he nervously delivered his adorable proposal speech.

I said "yes," and he slid the ring on my finger. I loved my ring and loved how my hand looked with it on my finger. But the moment I said yes, I paused. *But I thought we were going to wait. This isn't the right time. We're not okay.* I dismissed the thoughts as quickly as they had come. I didn't want anyone else. I only wanted Steve, and even though things weren't great, I couldn't imagine my life without him.

CHAPTER 9

CHILD PORN AND
A WEDDING

B Y THE TIME I TRANSFERRED to the Electronic Crimes Task Force (ECTF), I had developed a decent reputation in the office. Agents and supervisors would describe me as a team player, a hard worker, a good person, and someone who took pride in my work. I was happy that I was able to prove myself in the office. Occasionally a senior agent or supervisor would treat me dismissively for my lack of experience or age (maybe even my gender). But for the most part, I don't think there were many people who disliked me. I tried not to give them a reason to dislike me.

It wasn't long after I joined ECTF that I realized how genuinely good many of the members were. It was a great group of mostly men and a couple of women. I hadn't worked with other law-enforcement agencies very much in Bank Fraud, but I loved working with the other investigators. The squad was tight, and that elevated morale.

When I had first gotten to the squad, I was assigned a couple of fraud cases that, as usual, wound up going nowhere. Peer-to-peer file sharing software like LimeWire was part of a lot of the cases in ECTF at the time. Most remember LimeWire as a way to download music, but you downloaded with a hope and a prayer that a virus didn't accompany the latest hit song you didn't purchase like you were supposed to. But nonmusical files were also shared between users, including stolen PII, or personal identifying information. In other words, identity theft cases.

But aside from the agency mission of financial crime investigations, there was another type of investigation that drastically changed my life: child pornography investigations.

Porn, in general, is a controversial topic. The Secret Service is definitely responsible for my first real exposure to it was when I started ECTF at age twenty-five. I definitely did not become a Secret Service agent because I wanted to work child-porn cases. I never thought I would ever see child pornography. I grew up in a Christian home, and other than the obligatory "birds and the bees" talks, there wasn't much discussion about sex in general except that it was a sin before marriage.

I was neither married nor a virgin when I started working child pornography cases, but I didn't get around sexually prior to being with Steve. The shy girl with an ugly Speedo and goggle tan line who never developed decent boobs didn't exactly have a ton of suitors knocking at her door.

I had never intentionally watched porn before those cases. It just wasn't something I sought out. I'd encountered it unintentionally from time to time. But in ECTF, I had to see normally pleasurable acts being done to or by children, images I desperately wanted to turn away from but had to document for investigative purposes.

The first time I had seen child porn, I had to excuse myself for a few minutes after we prepared the initial case paperwork. I felt a tragic combination of sadness and nausea. I didn't know if crying or vomiting would have made me feel better. Those images don't leave minds when the photos and videos disappear. It was not exactly something I could go home and discuss and process over dinner and definitely not something I could process with my married male colleagues.

I inwardly cringed when well-meaning friends would ask about work.

"What kinds of cases are you working right now, Mel?"

"I'm working in a cyber squad right now, so that kind of stuff." *Please don't ask me any more questions.*

"Oh, really? Like hacking?"

"Sometimes, but I mostly work cases with peer-to-peer file sharing. It's kind of boring," I'd lie about the boring part, hoping they'd get bored with the conversation too.

"You mean where people trade illegal music?"

"Yeah." *Come on, Mel. Think of something interesting to change the topic.*

"But why are you working those kinds of cases as a Secret Service agent?"

"Since it's a task force, we work a lot of different types of cases." *It's about to get awkward.* "But right now I'm mostly working child pornography cases." *Wait for it. Aw, yes. There it is: the look of disgust.*

"Oh, gosh, nobody wants to hear about that stuff." *I know. Most people don't want to see it either.*

"Yes, it's pretty awful." *Stop looking at me like that. I'm not the monster. You don't know what I had to see just today. I had to document a play-by-play of a toddler being forced to give a blow job to a creepy middle-aged man or two little girls pretending sex with another adult male was a fun game. These are the tame ones, sadly. You definitely don't want to hear about the five-year-old anal close-up.*

"I don't know how you refrain from castrating them when you arrest those guys," they'd say. *Arresting them is satisfying until we go back to the office and find too many potential cases and not enough time to actually make a dent in the problem.*

"I wish it were possible to get rid of it altogether. You have no idea," I'd answer honestly. *You're giving me that look again. This stuff exists no matter how hard you try to shelter yourself from it.*

"Well, it was nice to see you. I've got to make a call," they'd awkwardly say, looking around the room for someone else to talk to. *Yeah, I'm sure you do.*

We didn't talk about the cases much in the squad either. Perhaps it was because I was usually one of the only female agents around. There was a particularly violent video found by one of the forensic analysts during a computer exam. While it was not discussed in detail with me personally, the examiner claimed it was one of the worst he'd seen. The details were hushed, and I'd felt bad for him. He had a wife and kids at home. I'm sure he didn't become a Secret Service agent because he wanted to examine pedophile computers all day.

I have a lot of respect and sympathy for other law enforcement and public service entities that work sexual crimes outside the computer. When the victims are actually in front of you, I imagine the emotional decompression can be excruciating.

I found the search warrants to be especially difficult because they usually involved interviews and identifying the suspect in the case. I sat in on a lot of interviews, probably because I had better handwriting for note taking than most of the guys. The warrants drained me. Hearing about the deep, dark secrets and closet addictions that destroyed families and other relationships made my head spin. Obviously, it helped our cases if the suspect confessed, but sometimes we minimized the crime to get the confession.

"It's not like you're the one who filmed it. You just downloaded it and let others download it from you."

During one search warrant, a bestiality video was playing on the computer as we made the initial entry. During another search warrant, the wife of the suspect denied knowing about her husband's computer activities. It was sometimes hard to read the reactions of family members when the nature of our warrant was revealed. Most of the time, they were very quiet. They'd usually deny any knowledge of their roommate or family member's sex and computer habits, but I often suspected they did know or at least had suspicions.

No matter how many cases we worked, there were twenty more to take its place. And our cases were just child-porn possession and distribution cases. Even if the person producing and filming the actual porn were caught, eliminating the files from the internet was pretty much impossible.

Rather than discuss any of that in great detail with Steve, I'd tried to focus on the stuff he was interested in, like how the warrants went.

"Were you in the stack this time?" he'd ask. The stack is the line of law enforcement that makes the initial entry and clears the building before the search begins.

"Did you find any weapons? How did you clear the building?" He liked to discuss the tactical stuff.

The squad had a tradition after warrants: breakfast. Since search warrants were usually executed early in the morning, it was late morning when we finished, and stomachs were growling. A couple of agents would take the evidence back to the office while the rest of us decompressed over coffee and something scrambled or jellied. I always found the scene of a bunch of law-enforcement officers laughing and teasing each other over breakfast an awkward one. I wondered if anyone felt guilty for having a good time after what we'd just had to see and discuss. I realize now that it was probably just our way of grasping some sense of normalcy after the most abnormal of mornings, our way of taking our minds off earlier events. But there was nothing normal about discussing pedophile fetishes as the sun came up.

It's been said that the toughest of jobs often have to be carried out by the strongest of people. I think it takes a strong person to maintain composure and sanity while working crimes against children, but I think strong people often have a hard time admitting their mental and emotional strength needs time to recover and reenergize.

Working in ECTF helped me find my switch. I figured out what I needed to do to turn off my heart and focus on the work. I suppressed my natural response to something I found repulsive, and it became easier to leave the "I'm okay" switch on in other aspects of my life. Suppression dulls emotions after a while, and I became proficient at suppressing what bothered me in general.

My suppression would catch up with me in time. Just as not taking accrued vacation or sick leave very often became a way of life, I chose to blatantly lie to myself and others about how I was really doing with all the difficult situations at work… and about how dysfunctional I'd become outside of work.

As if my emotional roller coaster wasn't complicated enough, I was planning my wedding after child-porn search warrants and protection assignments. We had set a date at the end of April 2010, so the engagement was relatively short.

I was never the girl who kept a scrapbook for my future wedding. I didn't know what kind of dress I wanted. I didn't know the difference between the colors ivory and pearl. I didn't know if I wanted to have a themed wedding. I didn't know what went into planning a wedding or all those wedding etiquette rules. My sister was the one to fill me in, and I followed her suggestions.

To this day, my family says our wedding was one of their favorites. We had a great DJ who had brought out the crazy and wild side of some of the quieter family members (and we had a dry wedding). All my bridesmaids said I was not a bridezilla. My childhood neighbor made beautiful lily centerpieces for the tables. Our wedding favors were homemade chocolate-chip cookies. I was overwhelmed at the love that went into making that day special for us.

While the wedding was perfect, I was a wreck inside. I

couldn't sleep the night before because my mind was racing. Why was I so nervous? Was I having second thoughts, or were those feelings normal? My stomach was in knots during hair and makeup the next morning.

Steve's family was mostly uninvolved in the planning of the wedding. His parents hadn't been in contact for a few years until our wedding, so I knew the reunion might be awkward for them. I had told myself the totality of the circumstances was making me tense but it was normal and no reason for alarm.

Steve reserved a cottage at a bed-and-breakfast in Big Bear for the weekend. Our wedding was on a Friday, so we drove up the mountain after the wedding in his brother's truck because Steve wanted to go off-roading. By that time, I wasn't feeling well. I hadn't eaten much all day, and I'd been in the hot wedding dress for hours. Ants had crawled up my wedding dress and legs during the outdoor pictures, and I was itchy and fatigued. We'd stopped for gas and those awful energy drinks on the way up the mountain, and I drank one hoping it would perk me up. This was my wedding night, after all. I wasn't supposed to be sick.

After we had checked into the bed-and-breakfast, Steve got a call from his family saying his grandma was in the hospital. She'd danced and had so much fun at the wedding. She was so cute! But she had a ministroke called a TIA afterward. Steve was ready to drive back down the mountain to the hospital, but his family reassured him that she was okay.

We'd decided to take a shower. I had started feeling dizzy shortly after the hot water hit me. I vaguely remember calling Steve's name. The next thing I remember was Steve shaking my shoulders gently as I regained consciousness. Thankfully, he caught me before I hit my head.

"Mel, we are going to the Urgent Care now. You fainted." He pulled me to my feet and steadied me until I could stand on my own. I felt terrible. This was not how wedding nights were supposed to go. After a minute or two though, I felt much better.

"Please, Steve. I'm okay. I didn't eat very much today, and

the dress was really hot when we were outside taking pictures. I probably just need to eat and drink something. Please. I'm so sorry. I'm okay. Really. I'm okay."

It took some convincing, but he finally relented. We'd spent most of our wedding night sitting in the Big Bear Denny's (the closest place that was open) eating grilled cheese and fries. I was fine the next morning, and we went off-roading and exploring for the weekend.

The week after the wedding, we had the biggest fight we'd ever had. It was about the same old stuff: me working too much and him not trying to find a job. The end result was crying and yelling on my part, and I'd known that only solidified my naivety and resolved nothing. I assumed being married would fix the problems. I hadn't handled it in an effective or meaningful way. I know that now. My marriage didn't start very honeymoon-like.

But my usual habits continued. I went back to work, and our home life remained the same. I suppressed what I was feeling, and as long as I didn't boil over in emotion and anger or bring up a serious conversation at home, we got along. Steve never initiated a tough discussion, and the resentment was only growing… for both of us.

CHAPTER 10

THE BLURRY
YEARS

'VE HEARD PEOPLE TALK ABOUT blackout periods or blocks of time in the past that seem to be forgotten. I imagine those periods usually revolve around tragedy, trauma, or tough circumstances. Even though I tend to be skeptical of people who say they simply "don't remember," it's understandable that trying to forget the past can be much easier than remembering it. We choose how we recall events, whether conscious or subconscious, and I'd venture to guess it's easier to focus on the parts that hurt the most. As Edgar Allan Poe once wrote, "Years of love have been forgot, in the hatred of a minute."

After the wedding, I went into a survival mode of sorts. Much of 2010, 2011, and some of 2012 are very blurry to me now. I can list what happened during those years in bullet point form like a to-do list, but I was mostly emotionally checked out. That switch was on, but no one was home.

Steve continued to work as a reserve officer. He worked a couple of shifts each week for a while and eventually started getting paid for it. When we were together, our time consisted mostly of my getting home from work and cooking, cleaning, and doing laundry followed by a shower and maybe catching up on a television show until I couldn't keep my eyes open. Then we'd go to bed, he'd put my hand on his head as if to ask for a head rub, and I'd fall asleep thirty seconds later only to have my alarm go off at five a.m. (or earlier) for a search warrant or some other assignment.

It's not like we hated each other. We were actually developing quite a talent at getting along despite our issues. If we kept conversations light and fun, it was a happy home.

One night we both woke to a loud clanging sound outside. It sounded like someone either ran into our back gate or slammed it loudly.

"Did you hear that?" I asked.

"Yeah, I think someone might be in the back yard," he said as he reached into the closet for his gun and flashlight. I grabbed mine too and was right behind Steve as he got to our bedroom door. I reached up and squeezed his shoulder, and we proceeded to quickly clear the house like it was a search warrant. When we had gotten to the back door where we could see the yard and gate, nothing looked out of the ordinary.

"See anything?" I whispered.

"Nothing. But that wasn't the wind moving the gate. It was something big."

After a moment, we heard the gate clanging and shaking again. As we stood there with our guns—both of us in our underwear—a large raccoon climbed over the gate and headed toward the road.

"You've got to be kidding me," I said as we watched the critter clumsily climb the gate in the noisiest manner possible. We chuckled and made our way back to the bedroom.

As we secured our guns and flashlights, Steve looked up at me and said, "You squeezed my shoulder when you came up behind me." A lot of law-enforcement agencies have their entry teams "squeeze up" from the back to the front to let the guy in front know the team is ready to go.

"Yeah, I guess I did."

"That was awesome," he said with a little gleam in his eye.

"We just stacked up and cleared our house like Mr. and Mrs. Smith for a stupid raccoon." I laughed.

After a handful of more difficult site and transportation advances, I was finally assigned my first lead advance—the agent who coordinates and oversees the security plan for a visit—in November 2010 when former president George W. Bush stopped in Los Angeles during a book tour. We took him to *The Tonight Show* with Jay Leno and to the Reagan Presidential Library in Simi Valley, CA. It was at the Reagan Library that I first saw former First Lady Nancy Reagan as Bush escorted her into the venue and to her seat. She was still walking then, but slowly. As a former First Lady, she was still entitled to Secret Service protection, and she had a small detail in the swanky Bel Air neighborhood of Los Angeles.

The visit went well, and the supervisors assigned to the visit seemed pleased. I was happy to have a lead advance under my belt. In a large office like the Los Angeles Field Office, it was harder to get them. Agents in smaller offices like the Midwest often got much more protection advance experience earlier in their careers than the larger offices because so many agents were in the mix and needed the experience. It was a wait-your-turn mentality in Los Angeles.

I was not selected for the Rescue Swimmer course in 2010 or 2011. But I kept swimming. My tryout times were always ranked higher than the agents my office selected, but seniority seemed to win in the end. All but one quit or failed the course. There was another agent in the office also trying to get into the course, a former NCAA Division I swimmer named Colin. He and I were both hired in 2007, and he was still ridiculously fast and consistently posted the fastest tryout times year after year. Still every year neither of us was chosen, and I was growing frustrated. That course was really the one thing I absolutely had to do, and I was going to keep trying until I did.

It was during that blurry time that headquarters sent a solicitation for volunteers to go to the Vice Presidential Protective Division (VPD). The solicitation applied to agents who were hired in 2007 like me. It was a great option for agents who wanted to leave the field early and move on to their protection detail requirement (referred to as Phase 2). But many agents wanted to hold out for the Presidential Protective Division (PPD) because they thought it would be better for their careers. VPD was sometimes referred to as the JV Team, as if being on VPD was a punishment and PPD (the Big Show) was where they sent the most squared-away agents.

A lot of PPD agents will claim only the best went to PPD, but any honest agent would admit that sometimes protection assignments were assigned based on the "needs of the Service," a phrase every agent knew well. If the agency had a need (like more agents on VPD), then it would be filled with the next agent on deck for Phase 2 or the first to volunteer. A lot of agents wanted to be on VPD because they wanted to avoid the drama and micromanaging that sometimes plagued PPD. That's not to say PPD was a bad place to be. Everyone had a preference and probably a legitimate reason for wanting a particular protection assignment.

When the solicitation for VPD came out, I was very torn. It forced a long overdue conversation between Steve and me, but we both knew I had signed a Mobility Agreement, meaning I acknowledged that I would likely be required to relocate one or more times throughout my career. When I signed it when I had gotten hired, I had every intention of relocating for protection, or Phase 2.

But now I was married, and I was married to someone who ultimately did not want to move to DC. And I loved Los Angeles and still do. I was torn because I was doing well at work, and aside from the child-porn investigations, I loved the job. When I was discouraged because of child-porn investigations, I would find my spirits lifted after a protection assignment. Driving in the motorcades and wearing my badge and lapel pin with pride during a protection assignment, no matter how small, was the adrenaline rush that reminded me why I wanted this job. My work mattered. It was my validation.

Deep down, I really wanted to volunteer for the VPD assignment. Maybe a change of scenery would be good for both of us, I had reasoned. Maybe a new city and environment was what we needed.

Steve was never willing to relocate for my job. He never said, "Mel, I don't have a full-time job. The job market is very competitive for me right now. If we're going to make the move to DC for a few years, maybe now is the time to do it. I will try to find another law-enforcement job in DC."

I really resented him for it. I was mad that he expected me to continue to be the primary financial support and responsible adult in the marriage. I was mad he wanted to have a baby as soon as possible because he thought he was ready to be a dad. I resented him for being okay with holding me back career-wise so he could indefinitely wait for what he wanted.

That was how I saw our situation at the time. While some of the frustration and anger might have been justified, I played the victim because it was easier than owning my part in our strained relationship. I'm not proud of that.

Ultimately, I made the decision not to volunteer for the vice president's detail.

I was not fully honest with Steve because I was afraid moving to DC would be the beginning of the end for us. He would never forgive me for taking him away from his family and friends and putting him in a position where he might have to go through another law-enforcement academy. I didn't realize it then, but I felt guilty for my success. I thought it was making him feel bad about himself or inadequate. I never wanted to bring him down, but I'm sure suppressing my real feelings and eventually lashing out via angry outbursts were anything but uplifting no matter where my heart was.

A few of my classmates volunteered for VPD, and I was jealous when their transfer orders came out. I told myself that life was more than this job, and I had to think about what Steve wanted too. At the time, there were two California-based protection details, former First Lady Nancy Reagan's in Los Angeles and former First Lady Betty Ford's in the Palm Springs area. If I could get on one of those details, Steve and I wouldn't need to move out of California for Phase 2. That would be a best-case scenario, I convinced myself.

I changed my preferences in my file and tried to put DC out of my mind. (At the time, agents weren't required to complete Phase 2 in DC. The current "needs of the Service" require DC protection time now.) As soon as I had changed my preferences, another advance and another ECTF warrant were waiting to keep me from dwelling on the decision.

Working child-porn cases in ECTF brought the idea of adoption into my head. Seeing so many children hurt and traumatized made me appreciate the upbringing I'd had. While my family was never perfect, I never doubted their love for me. I was protected from so much because they cared about me. While those children were being harmed and their innocence robbed, I was playing catch outside with my dad or riding bikes to the public swimming pool with my mom. Those kids had horrendous things to black out; my biggest trauma as a child revolved around losing my loose tooth in my breakfast cereal. How lucky I was to have parents who embodied the kindness and authenticity I wanted my life to also reflect.

Steve frequently told me, "I always knew I wanted to be a dad." I had managed to convince him to wait until we were both thirty. Yes, I was delaying. It wasn't that I didn't want kids, but I knew I definitely was not ready.

When I had asked Steve about adopting someday, he said, "I

want to have my own kids." I understood, and I wasn't upset about his desires. I was upset because he was so usually quick to say, "Mel, it's always your way or the highway with everything." It didn't seem like much was actually going my way at the time. But I loved the idea of helping a hurting child more than the idea of having my own. That sentiment hasn't changed.

I made a few great memories at work in May 2011 though. I'd been volunteering for pretty much every overseas protection assignment since I'd gotten out of training. I couldn't wait for an assignment in another country.

My first foreign trip was to Vancouver, British Columbia, for a former president Bill Clinton visit. It was an easy assignment, and I had a little time to explore. I ran along the Vancouver sea wall for miles and miles. I had to turn around because it started to rain, but I didn't care. It was beautiful to me even though I looked like a drowned rat when I'd gotten back to my hotel.

Less than a week after I'd returned from Vancouver, I flew to Washington DC and then flew in a military car plane to Dublin, Ireland, for President Obama's visit. I was scheduled to stand a post during the midnight shift at Obama's hotel. However, due to an Icelandic volcanic ash cloud, Obama did not stay overnight and avoided being grounded until the cloud had passed. Since my group had arrived a couple of days early for briefings, I spent several days in Dublin without actually working a single shift. I got the "bear" on that one.

Usually the most junior agents were assigned the midnight shift. It's typically viewed as a less desirable assignment. There were two other agents from Los Angeles on the trip with me, and they were both good guys. I'd learned to be careful on the road because many married male agents had the "wheels up, rings off" mentality. I was often the only female agent on trips, so I was grateful the Dublin trip had a couple of decent guys who were "safe" to hang out with as a married woman. They weren't going to try anything stupid.

We hit the town like tourists and saw as much as possible. We toured the Guinness brewery and the Jameson distillery. I'm not a big drinker, so that was more for the guys. We ate in the Temple Bar area, visited the cathedrals, and tried boxty, a potato pancake-type dish at the Boxty House.

Obama flew to Paris after Dublin, and my group leapfrogged to Warsaw, Poland, Obama's next stop after Paris. When we'd landed, Polish officials made a spectacle of inspecting our passports as if we were up to something sketchy. It was hard not to chuckle because it was not like the president's visit was a secret.

After the briefings, we visited the Warsaw Uprising Museum, the Pawiak Prison Museum, and found the remaining portion of the Warsaw Ghetto wall.

My favorite spot in Warsaw was the Old Town Market Square. Various shops, restaurants, and street vendors competed for our attention. We ate dinner in the outdoor seating area within the square's courtyard. There was no sense of urgency that night, and I savored the rare opportunity to enjoy rather than scarf a meal, a concept foreign to many Secret Service agents living an on-the-go lifestyle. It's sad that I remember those meals mostly because I remember being relaxed, something that didn't happen often apparently.

At some point during that mostly blurry time, I was notified of pending openings on former First Lady Betty Ford's protection detail near Palm Springs and former First Lady Nancy Reagan's detail in Los Angeles. Since both were on my preferences, I waited to see if I would get transfer orders. I didn't. As expected, those transfers went to agents more senior to me. Mrs. Ford passed away in July 2011, so even if I did get transferred, it would have been short-lived.

The day Mrs. Ford died, I had received instructions to pack a bag and drive to Palm Springs because I was being assigned the lead advance for George W. Bush again. He was scheduled to attend Mrs. Ford's funeral.

All living former First Ladies as well as the current First Lady Michelle Obama attended the service. Nancy Reagan asked Bush to escort her into the church because she was still a bit unsteady on her feet.

The advance agents coordinated having the motorcades arrive around the same time with Bush arriving first to meet Mrs. Reagan. She looped her arm through his, and I led them to the elevator.

"Good to see you, Nancy," Bush said. "I'm glad to see you've still got your wits about you."

Mrs. Reagan gave him a death glare for a second before responding. "Well, I certainly hope so," she said with a hint of annoyance.

He chuckled and away we went.

In true comedic fashion (but not comedic at the time), I hit the wrong button on the elevator, and we went to the wrong floor. The door opened to caution tape and signs saying the obvious: we were not supposed to be there. I was mortified. This was not a mistake a lead agent made and definitely not one I made. After all, I'd been responsible for preparing and securing the movements of Bush. I'd been there all week, and I hit the wrong button.

Bush didn't help matters either, saying, "I think we're in the wrong place" followed by his signature "hehe" chuckle we have all probably heard a time or two on the TV. I looked back and quickly apologized to the protectees and the Secret Service supervisors staring at me. Bush was still chuckling at my blunder, but Mrs. Reagan was not. She gave me an ever-so-slight eyebrow raise but said nothing.

It was in that instant that I realized she scared me. The power emulating from that small figure was intimidating.

A couple of months later, I got another lead advance at the United Nations General Assembly in New York City. I was assigned to Prime Minister Iveta Radicova of Slovakia. She was one of those protectees many didn't recognize because when she wasn't going to official functions, she was in jeans and a T-shirt, walking through toy stores and other shopping venues.

The advance went way too smoothly. My NYPD motorcade counterparts were hilarious. Both of them worked together and had been cops for many years. "Seasoned" is probably the best descriptor. One of the guys was a big jolly cop with the New York attitude to match. The other guy was smaller with an even bigger attitude. They embodied my idea of cool kids. They didn't get frazzled about anything.

We sat down for our initial meeting, and the big dude said, "Hey, our brass doesn't want us meeting up with our counterparts yet, but that's stupid. We gotta prepare, so screw them. But maybe don't mention that we met up."

"Okay. We've just met and we already have secrets. Nice to meet you, gentlemen." I laughed and we went on with our plans.

The Secret Service uses phrases like putting out fires because that's what the work felt like sometimes, especially at UNGA. The most prepared agents could wind up with the biggest mess of a visit, especially if the foreign staff didn't communicate or follow security protocols, leaving everyone feeling like soup sandwiches despite all the work.

The Secret Service supervisor assigned to the Slovakian detail was one of my academy instructors and coincidentally one the instructors who had overseen the protection portion of training. No pressure. We'd nicknamed him Extreme Cage Fighter in training because he was big, bald, and had a goatee. He kind of looked like an old-school pro wrestler.

The first couple of days of the visit went well. My NYPD counterparts drove through the NYC streets like professionals, clearing pedestrians with ease. Since New Yorkers are not known to be the most respectful of law enforcement, these guys sometimes had to rely on their aggressive driving more than their lights and sirens.

"Hey, genius!" one would yell at a pedestrian trying to cut through the motorcade. "Don't you see we've got a dignitary here? Wait your turn, yeah?"

"Everyone's a dignitary this week, idiot," retorted some random local.

One night after all the official meetings were over, the prime minister wanted to go to a Czech restaurant for dinner. As she ate, we took turns getting food in the basement area of the restaurant. I went outside to relieve one of the drivers because we couldn't just park and come inside. Nothing could be left unattended, not just the protectee.

"Hey, man. There's some food downstairs. Go eat. I'll watch the car."

"Thank you," he said as he climbed out of the car. "How's it looking in there?"

"She's still eating. Not looking like we're leaving anytime soon."

"Awesome. Be back in a bit."

No sooner had he walked into the restaurant than my clumsy self bumped the car door and sent it flying shut. I pulled the handle. Nothing. I'd just locked the keys in the protectee's car. The spare key was also in the car, and in Astoria, we were too far away from the hotel in the Upper East Side to retrieve the other spare keys.

That was a bad scenario and evidence of poor planning on my part. I should have had another spare key in my pocket. Now, as the lead advance, I had to fix the problem. I tried to remain calm, but I was scared, my mind running with a million ways it could turn out very badly.

I got the attention of the NYPD officers who were stuffing their faces while they could.

"Um, guys. Any chance you have a Slim Jim in the trunk of the patrol car?"

"What's going on?" one of them asked between bites.

"I just locked the keys in the car."

"Don't you have a spare?" Fair question.

"It's also in the car."

"Shit."

"Yeah, I know."

They looked in their unit and came back empty-handed. There were no other cops nearby. One of the shift agents had come outside to see if I'd eaten yet. I told him what was going on and asked him to please (please, please) keep me posted on what was happening inside.

"We may need to stall her if she wraps this up in the next five minutes."

"Hey, I know a guy in this precinct," the shorter cop said with the coolest NYC accent as he walked up to me. He got on his phone, and before I knew it, an NYPD truck, an Emergency Services Unit (their SWAT), came rolling around the corner with lights flashing.

"Oh my God, please tell them to turn off the lights," I whispered, but he was way ahead of me on his radio and the lights turned off. The truck parked down the street, and some officers walked up with a couple of tools. They had the car door open in five seconds. It was about as inconspicuous as it could have been. I have never been so relieved. I ran to the lead NYPD vehicle and pulled out my swag bag. Most agents have a swag bag with token lapel pins, challenge coins, or other trinkets to give or trade. I took the whole bag and handed it to the group of NYPD officers in the truck.

"Here. Take it all. You saved me tonight. I can't thank you enough." I was ashamed I didn't have more to offer them in addition to the countless "thank yous" and "you saved me tonights." To the best of my knowledge, no one other than those few officers and a couple of agents ever knew what had happened. We certainly agreed to say our grateful prayers and not tell the detail leader. This would stay a "need to know" situation. Crisis averted.

Aside from learning to always have extra spare keys, I realized I wasn't invincible no matter how hard I worked or thought I'd prepared. I was a control freak with my protection assignments. I never wanted to be the reason anything went wrong. Maybe some of my clumsiness could be tamed, but knocking that door shut and needing to ask for help to fix it was incredibly humbling.

Despite the big learning points of the Slovakian lead advance, the highlight of that assignment was when my Blackberry buzzed in my pocket during the advance. Instead of another schedule update from my embassy contact, it was a notification that I was being reassigned to the Protective Intelligence squad in the Los Angeles Field Office when I returned from my assignment in New York.

The relief I felt cannot be expressed in words. I wanted out of the child-porn investigations. In reality, I needed out, but I didn't realize how badly at the time.

I may remember most of those blurry years in blotchy spurts, but I vividly remember leaving New York City in September 2011 with a relieved smile on my face.

CHAPTER 11

THE CRAZIES AND A CAMPAIGN ASSIGNMENT

THE PROTECTIVE INTELLIGENCE (PI) SQUAD in Los Angeles worked threat cases. If someone sent a letter or email to the White House that originated in the Los Angeles district, my new squad would investigate it. Sometimes concerned citizens would call about a Facebook post they'd seen. Other times law enforcement would have someone in custody who'd said something threatening. Cases originated in all sorts of ways.

The squad was small when I got there, so we were busy and took turns working the in-town protection visits. Obviously PI agents were involved in all the visits to monitor any potential threats. The work, in general, was more serious due to the investigations being intelligence related, but the squad members themselves were a good group but in a different, more structured way than ECTF.

The office had regular local "lookouts" of frequent callers (sometimes called the "crazies"). If they had a negative direction of interest toward a protectee, then their picture would be plastered all over briefing PowerPoints before protection assignments.

The PI squad was monitored by upper management a lot, and that led to feelings of being micromanaged at times. There is a fine yet slightly fuzzy line between free speech and a threat. Just because someone disliked a protectee didn't make him or her a lookout for the PowerPoint. The muddiest area would be what we called a veiled threat. Posting "Someone should put a bullet in the president" is one example. The person isn't saying they are going to hurt anyone, but they probably wouldn't be sad if someone else did. Merely saying or writing you want to harm a protectee is a violation of federal law. There doesn't have to be an overt act in furtherance of the crime like in, for example, a fraud case. Posting something like "I'm going to bomb the White House" could potentially get you arrested.

Speaking of bombing the White House, most of our cases were pure crap. That's good, actually. There was a lot of time spent eliminating threats, meaning a tip would come in, and we were thankfully able to investigate enough to say that person didn't have a high potential for a negative outcome against a protectee. Those cases often led to some frustration and even humor. At one point, a local high school student posted that he was going to bomb the White House. It wasn't my case, but I went for the interview when he got pulled out of class.

"Woooooooow," he said with a dumbfounded look as he sat down and started fidgeting with the edge of his shirt. "You guys actually came."

My partner was not amused in the moment, but we had a good laugh out of imitating him later. Apparently, his class had a guest speaker who'd said the government monitored internet traffic. The speaker told the class if someone posted online that they were going to blow up the White House, the Secret Service would come and arrest them. Well, this idiot decided to test it out. He wasn't an actual threat, but the post itself meant we had to make sure.

My very first interview in the PI squad was quite enlightening and definitely reflective of my lack of understanding when it came to mental illness. I am ashamed to say I was judgmental of many who claimed to be suffering from mental illness, assuming that personal weakness probably contributed to the alleged diagnoses. It should not come as any surprise that I made those assumptions though. I subscribed to the "suck it up" line of thinking. Sometimes bad things happened and you had to deal with it. Get it together, people. It's cringe-worthy to even admit it now.

I conducted my first interview after I had gotten a call from headquarters about numerous handwritten letters received by the White House from someone in our district. The writer wrote maniacally and nonsensically. The postmark and return address came back to Norwalk, CA. The letters had the "magic words" with phrases about killing the president and bombs sprinkled between nonsense.

The letter sender was at the Metropolitan State Hospital in the wing for the criminally insane. It was my first time in a mental hospital. The door to the wing swung open to another long hallway with patient rooms. At the end of the hall was a nurse's station. It was circular-shaped and encased in glass or Plexiglas windows giving them a 360-degree view of the common area and a good view of most of the hallway.

As we walked, a patient popped out of his room and pointed down the hall, repeating the phrase, "She's over there." My eyes widened a bit, and I walked faster. Toward the end of the hall, another patient popped out and said, "Hey, I just threw my chair out the window." A quick glance in his room revealed nothing of the sort.

No sooner had we closed the door to the nurse's station than two other patients in the common area started fighting. A group of staff and orderlies rushed the fighting duo, and I realized I was definitely out of my element. During the whole incident, I noted a small man at a table with his back to me. He had a stack of white papers and another stack of envelopes with a few pencils next to him. He was completely oblivious to what was going on around him as he scribbled on the pages.

"I'm pretty sure that's our guy," I said as I pointed to the quiet man after greeting the nurses. The charge nurse told me this patient wrote letters to government agencies all day every day. Per policy, the hospital mailed the letters written by patients.

When I approached the man and introduced myself, he popped up excitedly.

"I'm so glad you're here. I've been waiting for you." He asked us to sit down so we could talk.

Most of his words were incoherent, and I felt bad for him after a few minutes. He was smiling and seemed happy to see us. What I was able to glean from his ramblings was that he was warning the government about the voices he was hearing. The voices were telling him to blow up the White House and harm the president. When he said he wouldn't do it, "they" blew air in his belly button, and "it really hurt."

"I would never hurt anyone," he kept saying. "But I must warn you. Please don't let anything happen to the president."

That interview made me realize there are a lot of people who are legitimately sick, and my prior judgment was horribly ignorant. How little I knew about mental illness. I arrogantly assumed people diagnosed with depression, bipolar disorder, and others were merely weak and incapable of handling life's troubles and difficulties. At least I don't have to take a pill. I'm sad and unhappy at home, but I'm not… crazy.

The scary part about the PI squad was that some legitimately sick people possessed the capabilities to carry out the threats they'd made. Many of the suspects were exceptionally intelligent. I felt like an idiot during a couple of interviews. I didn't have the wit or speedy brainpower to respond in kind. One of those hyperintelligent subjects of an investigation posted about me on his Facebook page. I came into the office a day or two after the interview, and my squad mates had printed out his recent posts and posted them on the bulletin board in our cubicle (highlighting the comments about me). Apparently, they got a kick out of the "lady agent" making an impression.

I loved working the protection visits as a PI agent. I got to work with local law enforcement a lot as we prepared for a dignitary or other protectee to visit the Los Angeles area. Since Los Angeles is a big tourist trap, there was never a shortage of in-town protection assignments with random foreign dignitaries. Driving in motorcades was fun, and Steve would say my face would light up when I talked about motorcade movements. My day-to-day work life significantly improved in the PI squad.

By 2012, the agency was gearing up for another chaotic presidential campaign year. There was a semicomplicated rotation of shifts set up. I was assigned to site and PI advances during my shift's rotation. Advance agents arrived days ahead of the protectee to set everything up. I primarily worked Presidential Candidate Mitt Romney's events that year with a few Vice Presidential Candidate Paul Ryan events.

That campaign year was an exceptionally busy one, but it was also my favorite. I learned a lot about protection away from the Los Angeles bubble. The quantity and variety of advances during rotations kept life interesting. At one point, I worked a PI advance for a Romney event at the Red Rock Amphitheater in Colorado, a famous outdoor venue with absolutely beautiful views. I advanced the Jacksonville Landing in Florida with another agent for a Romney/Ryan rally, and then I leapfrogged to Milwaukee for a Paul Ryan campaign advance. I wasn't as busy as some of the other campaign agents, but we often joked among each other on the road.

"What city are we in right now?" Those kinds of conversations would usually happen late at night over a meal at whatever restaurant was still open. I think I ate more fries in 2012 than I've ever eaten in my life.

"Dude, I don't even know anymore. It's hot and humid. We must still be in Florida." Of course it was a joke, but sometimes we were tired enough that slaphappy quips kept us sane.

Then the lead advance's phone would buzz and he'd sigh and look up at us. "Pack your bags, ladies and gentlemen. We are headed to Wisconsin tomorrow after wheels up. Hope you brought your coats because it's supposed to be cold."

Someone would moan and say, "I'm gonna need to find a place to buy a coat and warm socks. Crap. Now my bag is going to be overweight at the airport."

"Please tell me it's an in and out." (This means the protectee would fly in, attend an event, and then leave without spending the night.)

"You know it's not. We're not that lucky." The lead advance would probably sigh, and I'd steal someone's leftover fry as we paid the bill.

"I saw that." The fry victim would chuckle over his shoulder as we wearily walked back to the hotel. We complained to each other, but it was all in fun. When it was time to work, we hustled and got the job done.

However, while I was constantly traveling and constantly tired, Steve was at home. Even though we talked daily, I was not there, and the realities behind long bouts of separation are complicated. It's said that absence makes the heart grow fonder, but that's not a sustainable mindset and a dangerous concept to assume in any relationship. The reality was that absence forces independence, and as attached as I was to Steve, we were subtly creating our own separate lives while living under the same roof.

But unlike 2008, 2009, 2010, and 2011, I would finally get my chance at the US Secret Service Rescue Swimmer School in June 2012. I didn't even care that I had gotten my chance during the hectic schedule of a campaign year when training for the course would be difficult. I couldn't wait to go!

Colin, the fast swimmer in the Los Angeles office, was also selected. I'm pretty sure I squealed when I got the call from the main rescue swimmer instructors. Finally it was my turn.

CHAPTER 12

YOU HAVE
PLENTY OF AIR

WATER IS DANGEROUS EVEN WHEN it's calm and sleek as glass. It doesn't take much to disable even the strongest of men and women. It's an equalizer of sorts. For many, it instills fear, but what it really demands is respect. Panicking in water will virtually guarantee a negative outcome. Respect for the water is paramount to survival; work with it, and the odds increase.

I wasn't always respectful of the water or obsessed with swimming. In fact, getting me to swimming lessons as a child involved crying fits and whining. "I don't wanna go, Mommy. I don't wanna go." I'd scream through an entire lesson, and the teachers would tell my mom to keep bringing me back.

"You're going," she'd firmly say from the front seat of our old brown Suburban.

Finally, much to my parents' relief, one instructor name Ken (likened as a saint in the Lentz household) was able to get me to stop crying long enough to learn.

I became obsessed with swimming, however, when I was introduced to the 1992 Summer Olympic Games in Barcelona, Spain. At almost eight years old, I found myself glued to the TV, fascinated and thrilled. Janet Evans, my childhood hero, won the gold in the 800-meter freestyle. But it wasn't until I watched Summer Sanders win the gold medal in the 200-meter butterfly that I said to myself, "I want to be a swimmer."

I swam my little heart out every summer during swimming lessons. My sister and I would videotape swimming when it was on TV just so we could watch the races over and over again on VHS. I didn't start competing until high school though. I was never an Olympic-caliber swimmer, but I was all heart and never a quitter.

I fell in love with swimming around the same time I fell in love with the idea of being skinny and beautiful, a dangerous path for a young girl to travel. My swimming career in high school and college was a picture of personal negligence and the resiliency of the body under the guise of youth.

Many don't know about my eating disorder history. They know about my love for swimming. I was one of those crazy kids who couldn't wait for practice and was so excited to start swimming "doubles" or two-a-day practices. I thought I was going to get so much faster with the extra training. I did improve despite the beginning of disordered eating.

It started as just a "harmless" diet, a desire to get a little skinnier. I wasn't overweight to begin with. But it turned into something bigger in a hurry. Swimming became a means of burning calories, and food became the enemy. While I'd thought I had unlimited energy, I had trouble sleeping and, most annoyingly, constantly felt cold.

I lied to my family about my eating habits—something I felt incredibly guilty for—and tried to convince them that my weight loss was because I was exercising a lot and wanted to swim in college.

"Of course I ate lunch. I eat three meals a day. I'm just

exercising a lot, that's all." I'd lie through my teeth.

Loving someone with an eating disorder has to be very hard. The helplessness my family must have felt as they tried to help me. I pushed my family away with lies and destructive behaviors. They told me I was beautiful all the time. I knew I could go to them with a problem, but I chose not to, and it hurt more than just myself.

I was selected for the 2012 Rescue Swimmer course in March or early April 2012. The course itself was in June. So that meant I had about two months to get into shape for it. Colin and I talked to the other rescue swimmers in our office to get training tips. The more I asked around, the more frustrated I became. The course seemed to have a lot of secrets, and I got a lot of vague and general tips.

"Practice a lot with the fins."

"Do a lot of underwater swimming." I was already good at lung busters, as many swimmers call them, so I did even more of them.

Those tips were the extent of their assistance. I didn't know it until I got to the course, but without exception, every other swimmer there had gotten way more guidance and pool time with rescue swimmers in their offices. Maybe the Los Angeles rescue swimmers were legitimately busy. It was a campaign year after all. If not, maybe they simply had thought I wouldn't make it and wasn't worth the effort.

Even though I hadn't been purging since Steve and I got together, I still struggled with the negative self-talk and excessive mirror time or time spent looking at myself, pinching at "fat," and analyzing what needed shrinking. I knew it bothered Steve, and he sometimes mentioned that I should go talk to someone about these lingering issues.

"I swear to God, if you pinch at your stomach one more time, I'm going to take all the mirrors out of this house," he'd threaten. My issues usually came up during arguments.

"You want me to help you around the house and act more like a husband, but I've asked you many times to go talk to someone about your body issues, and you never follow through," he'd say.

"Well, you know how many times I've been asking you for more sex? News flash, Steve: I really like sex with you. I'm not thinking about my body or those insecurities in those moments. It's probably the only time I'm not, and you know it. It's like you're punishing me. You're not doing my self-esteem any favors by making me feel undesirable."

And thus, the argument would go on until I started yelling and he refused to speak. Then we'd probably go to bed and pretend nothing happened the next day, or I would be the one apologizing for something nasty I'd said. Same story, different day. But in a way, he was right. I did need to address those lingering issues. I wish I had back then.

As I squeezed in training swims for the June 2012 course, I ate right and felt better than I ever did in high school or college. I was strong, and I was tired in a satisfying way and not a burned-out way. I was nervous but confident I was as ready as I was ever going to be.

I should mention I was selected for the class as the third alternate swimmer. Because of the high attrition, a few extra swimmers started the course but were not guaranteed a spot unless three people dropped out during the first part of training, known as pool week.

Colin and I were on the same flight to DC for the course. Our flight was delayed, and we didn't get to our hotel in Maryland until very late, probably after midnight. I was so nervous because I wasn't going to start day one on a good night's rest. I had been warned that the first week and a half was going to be the hardest part because it was designed to break us down and then make us quit before we went to North Carolina to train with the Coast Guard and Ocean Rescue.

The Secret Service Rescue Swimmer course is designed to

prepare agents to address a water-related emergency with a protectee. The agents are not trained to the extent of the Coast Guard Rescue Swimmers, but the Coast Guard was heavily involved in our training from the beginning.

After pool week, the class would go to Kitty Hawk, North Carolina, for surf training or ocean-based rescues where we'd learn Jet Ski rescues and how to read the water and spot rip currents, et cetera. After that, we would go to Elizabeth City, North Carolina, to train with the Coast Guard and practice open-water swimming and helicopter jumps and rescues. If we passed all that, we would go back to Maryland for swift-water training where local law-enforcement divers and swimmers taught us how to swim through rapids and make rescues in them. And finally, the last couple of days of the course consisted of all our final tests and scenarios. Mixed into all that was the medical portion known as WetMed.

WetMed was taught by medical professionals—paramedics and Johns Hopkins physicians—and was basically CPR, AED, First Aid, First Responder training in a wet and hazardous environment with a protection element. Essentially, the idea of triage was obsolete. Rescues focused on the protectees, not the other drowning staff, aides, or press. Everyone else would come second because our mission was to save the protectee.

The first thing we did on day one was the initial tryout again. I came in third in the distance swim behind Colin and another former NCAA Division I swimmer.

After the instructors had handed out all our gear for the course, we were instructed to line up at the deep end with all our gear on: snorkel, mask, fins, booties, wetsuit, gear vest, weight belt, carabineer, et cetera. Pool week was about to officially start.

The indoor pool, or training tank, looked like a giant warehouse attached to the building that housed the gym and mat rooms at Beltsville. The gym on the second floor had large windows overlooking the pool, giving RTC trainees and instructors a great view of our pain and suffering. On the opposite end of the pool was a giant contraption that mimicked a helicopter hoist. The platform was about twelve to fifteen feet high—close to level with the gym windows across the room— and had a hoist from an old helicopter where we would practice jumping, giving appropriate hand signals to the helicopter crew, and getting hoisted up properly.

Underneath the viewing room (gym windows) were the doors to the men's and women's locker rooms. No one was allowed to use the restroom alone, partly due to their emphasis on the buddy system but also because they didn't want someone passing out or having a medical issue in the bathroom alone.

Since that wasn't our first academy rodeo, it didn't take us long to figure out that the instructors demanded uniformity. We coordinated our moves quickly. We would walk with our fins, mask, and snorkel in our left hand. We would wear our shorty wetsuit, our booties (worn under the fins so we didn't get massive blisters), and our gear vest (full of gear like a CPR mask, lights, knife, whistle, et cetera). When we were instructed to take off all our gear, we would line everything up exactly the same way next to our feet every single time.

We were introduced to circuits on day one. They were tedious and designed to fatigue us while training us to complete random tasks underwater without panicking.

One of the lead instructors got on his megaphone and divided us into two groups: group one and group two. Then he bellowed, "Ones on the line, twos behind!" The twos stepped behind the ones.

"Listen up!" he said. "You will not pass this course if you cannot follow simple instructions."

I felt a hose spraying behind me. Another instructor was spraying us while we were standing there.

"At no time during these circuits should your snorkel ever come out of your mouth. Is that understood?"

"Yes, sir!" we all screamed through our snorkels, but it sounded garbled. A couple of instructors behind us chuckled.

Megaphone Man continued. "Swim under the rope at the bottom of the pool. Don't touch my rope. Surface swim the rest of the way. Come back underwater. Go under the rope. Do not touch my rope and get your ass back on the deck. Do not surface until you're done. Do not leave until you are instructed."

"Yes, sir!" we answered. More chuckles from instructors.

I was in group one, and we entered the water properly as instructed. I took a deep breath and dove underwater, taking great care to clear the rope that allowed for about two feet of clearance at the bottom of the pool. I saw the rope move; someone's fin had gotten snagged on it. I surfaced and swam to the other side. As I turned, I saw Colin ahead of me. We were ready for this. I went underwater again and cleared the rope, surfaced, pulled myself out of the water in one smooth motion, and got back in line, only to find the hose spraying in my snorkel as I was trying to breathe. But I didn't dare take the snorkel out of my mouth. I saw a couple of people in the twos pop up early.

When we were all back in line, Megaphone Man looked pissed.

"Who touched my rope?"

"Uh, it was me, sir," said a dejected-looking dude.

"Unbelievable. On your backs!"

We complied and waited for him to tell us what to do. The rope violator would lead the class cadence, and we did flutter kicks, an exercise performed in all our gear, including fins, and involved raising our legs up and down in an exaggerated flutter kick motion.

"Begin!" Megaphone yelled.

"One, two, three," the leader yelled in time with our leg movements.

"One!" the class would yell on the next beat.

"One, two, three."

"Two!"

"One, two, three."

"Three!" We'd continue the cadence until the instructor was good and ready to stop us. I was irritated I didn't have a six-pack at the end of the course after all those stupid flutter kicks.

"That's it! Ones on the line. Twos behind!" And we'd do it again and again.

Back and forth and back and forth. Other obstacles were added.

"Swim under my rope! Take off your weight belt and mask. Surface swim to the other side. Come back and put all your gear back on, clear your mask, and surface without touching my rope." That was one example, but they changed it up every time, and they added obstacles like rafts and ropes across the surface of the water.

During the first day, a few people were popping up early, clearly struggling with the underwater portion and dramatically sucking in air and taking their snorkels out of their mouths to get a breath. That did not go over well. As we did push-ups on the deck, Megaphone Man did more yelling.

"I don't understand why you can't follow simple instructions. I told you not to touch my rope, and you touched my rope. I tell you not to pop up early, and you can't hold your breath. Listen very carefully to what I am about to say. You have plenty of air! Someone will revive you if you don't. On your feet! Ones on the line, twos behind!"

Megaphone Man really meant the problem was often in our heads. Air is life, but panicking and surfacing when three to four more seconds of discomfort would complete the task didn't help anyone, including the future potential victims. In our case, the victim was the president or other protectee. The body and the mind can withstand just a little more discomfort if given enough credit to do so.

I made it through the first day without missing a single circuit or underwater swim. I was thankful for that. I hadn't caused any punishment on my first day. We were also quizzed on some WetMed, and I did well because I'd psycho-read the textbook about four times as I prepped for the course.

At the end of each day, we were assessed by all the instructors. There was a folding chair in the middle of their office, and the instructors would sit in a circle around each of us, one at a time. After the first day, they pretty much told us all we were useless and on the verge of going home. A couple did go home that day.

After we were released for the day, we all changed and met at our assigned vans to drive back to the hotel. We piled in, and as soon as the doors closed, someone said mockingly, "You have plenty of air guys. Someone will revive you." We laughed our butts off and said this to each other constantly throughout the course.

We stopped for dinner on the way back, looking like drowned rats in polo shirts as we got our food. We decided to eat in the lobby of the hotel. What a sight we must have been with our gear bags, wet hair, and ice packs on our swollen ankles from so much finning.

As I sat there with my dinner, I realized I was famished. I'd been in the water for about ten hours that day. Everyone was tired but trying to laugh and get to know each other better as they ate. I immediately thought back to dinners in the cafeteria after swim practice, the ones where I'd make an excuse to leave early so I could go purge in the science lab bathroom before the public safety officers locked it up for the night. All my destructive and deceptive habits came flooding back as I sat there staring at my dinner, my hands shaky from low blood sugar.

My negligence caught up with me my senior year of college, and I struggled from the beginning of the season. I had been compulsively exercising all summer, and I continued to purge normal amounts of food while thinking about how all the skinny, pretty girls with boyfriends at school only ate salad.

I could still hear my distance coach saying, "Mel, why are you going so slow?" at practice. That wasn't me. I was the training animal. Rather than admit my dirty little secret, my distance coach thought I needed additional training, so I got up earlier and started morning practice at five a.m. and joined the rest of the team when six a.m. practice started.

About midway through the season, my legs started turning numb and white during my races. I would have to sit on the pool deck for a minute until color returned and I could go warm down. I was never the star of the swim team, so it was easy to be invisible. Only a few swimmers saw or knew about my legs going numb and white during races. Distance swimmers are often overlooked because our races are long and usually unexciting.

Common sense would say to see a doctor, but I didn't. I was afraid they'd tell me to stop swimming. I couldn't let that happen, not during my senior year. I knew why all this was happening, and I just didn't want to admit it.

I barely made the team for the NAIA Nationals my senior year. I was scheduled to swim the 1,650-yard freestyle, 500-yard freestyle and the 200-yard butterfly. It's harder to be invisible at a championship meet. The school's head athletic trainer saw my legs after my first race. I wasn't able to stand up, and I was bad at faking the problem with, "Oh, I'm just resting a second." That time my fingers and forearms were also white.

"Mel, how long has this been going on?" she asked.

"A while now. It only happens when I race." The truth was it happened once in a while at practice too.

"Mel, this could be serious. You need to get this checked out."

My memories were interrupted by an outgoing rescue swimmer classmate.

"Guys, does anyone else feel like their face is getting bruised from wearing the mask all day?"

Someone answered, "Dude, that vest wore my neck raw."

"Well, maybe you should stop popping your neck up early during the underwater swims. Come on, man. You have plenty of air, remember?"

"Someone will revive you," I chimed in.

And then the conversation and laughter continued. No one said a thing about how much food I'd eaten, and I didn't gain a pound during the training. To top it off, the next morning, I felt awesome! Even though I was tired, I wasn't lethargic. My hands weren't shaky, and I wasn't going to let old swimming and eating habits creep into this course. Nope. Not this time.

Pool week continued with nonstop circuits followed by more underwater swimming and constant punishment for violations or errors. People were dropping like flies, either quitting or being volun-told to quit. By the second day, we'd already lost two or three people. We'd lose over one-third by the end of pool week. I was fretting about being an alternate for nothing. I was officially in the course within just a couple of days.

I was smaller than everyone else in the class except for the one other female named Kelly, a ridiculously strong woman. Having another female in the class was a huge blessing. It would have been very lonely in the locker room when the instructors yelled, "Hydrate! Urinate! Back on the deck in three minutes! Go!"

Kelly and I worked well together. We were not partnered for anything inside the pool, but we both went out of our way to encourage each other and keep each other going.

A couple of days into the school, Kelly and I figured out that if we worked together during our short three-minute breaks, we could actually accomplish a lot. We'd always drink water because all the swimming was dehydrating us, but we usually alternated between eating and peeing each break. If we both peed one break, we could help each other get our wetsuits off. During the next break, we'd stuff our faces. Although after a while, we just started peeing in the showers with our wetsuits on. Some people were probably peeing in the pool anyway. Gross.

One day in the locker room, I said to Kelly, "Don't you dare quit this course because I really don't want to have to sit in this locker room without you every day."

She laughed and we agreed we needed each other. We had this thing about yelling "I'm a LADY!" to each other in the locker room before we went back out to the pool deck. In between circuits and WetMed practice, we often practiced shark circles, drills where we wore blacked-out masks and the instructors would attack us so we could demonstrate proper escapes and releases without being able to see anything. For instance, if an instructor was being rough with us underwater during a scenario—holding us down and trying to get us to panic—we'd joke about it in the locker room, fanning ourselves in fake horror as we quipped, "Don't you try to drown me, sir. I'm a LADY!" Then we'd laugh and zip each other's wetsuits back up on our way to the training tank.

The instructors gave out the daily hammerhead award, an award given to whoever did the stupidest thing during the day. The recipient had to wear a lanyard with a plastic hammerhead shark on it everywhere he or she went. The lanyard part had SpongeBob SquarePants all over it. Some of us earned the hammerhead more than once, my first being when my vest got caught on the floating raft in the pool and inflated. There was a string of beads at the bottom of our gear vest. If the beads were pulled, the vest would inflate. Mine inflated as I pulled myself into the raft.

That, of course, happened in the middle of one of the circuits. Try as I might to get to the bottom of the pool to finish my task (getting my weight belt), I wound up inverted at the surface, my legs kicking in the air like a fool. Everyone had to do flutter kicks on the deck until I could get my vest deflated and complete the task.

"Ms. Lentz inflated her vest because she wasn't paying attention as she climbed into the boat! On your backs! You are all going to do flutter kicks until Ms. Lentz can get her act together. If she needed to dive underwater to rescue our protectee, I guess we'd just have a drowned president because Lentz decided to get careless with her gear!"

But no one in the class was mad at me in the end. Everyone had a hammerhead moment during the course. But the point was made: those kinds of mistakes couldn't happen in the real world.

We were a tight class, and even though we ached and hurt a lot, we were able to have fun together, mostly in the vans to and from training as we made fun of the instructors and each other. On the weekends, we were too tired to do anything but see pretty much every movie currently in theaters.

As the class got smaller and stronger, the instructors started messing with our gear during circuits, tying our weight belts into knots or switching our gear with someone else's entirely at the bottom of the pool while we were surface swimming.

On one particular day at the end of pool week (which was actually more than one week), the instructors tied my weight belt in knots *and* swapped all my gear with my swim buddy's. Any time we got caught wearing someone else's gear, it meant punishment and more circuits.

I was group one, and my swim buddy Sean was group two and followed when I was about halfway down the pool as instructed. I made the turn and saw the instructors tying a belt into a bunch of knots. They were right about where I had left my belt, so I assumed it was mine.

I took a deep breath before going down to retrieve my carabineer and my belt. I unscrewed the carabineer from the underwater rope, hooked it to my vest, and set out to untangle my belt. We were not allowed to surface until we had our gear back on. I untangled the belt and started to put it on at the bottom of the pool. As I was securing the buckle, I saw Sean's initials.

Ugh. Where did they put my belt?

I took the belt off underwater, waved to Sean, and pointed to his belt at the bottom of the pool. Then I started swimming around looking for my initials on a belt buckle. My lungs were burning, but I hadn't missed a circuit yet except for the inflated vest moment, and I didn't plan to start then. I found my belt, untangled multiple knots for what seemed like an eternity, and finally surfaced with my gear squared away. I climbed out of the pool, breathing heavily but refusing to act too dramatically about it. I got back in line, but everything was stinging and spinning. *You have plenty of air.*

"Holy shit, Lentz." I heard the lead instructor behind me who I didn't know had conveniently been standing over my lane watching my entire circuit. "Ho-ly shit."

That night, at my evaluation, the lead instructor said, "I don't know how long you were down there, but I don't think anyone else in the class could have done that."

"Yes, sir," was all I said, but I definitely let the grin peek out that day.

I didn't let it go to my head though. There was a lot of training left to do. But I slept like a baby that night, knowing I'd earned some respect from a bunch of protein-bar-eating dudes who had underestimated me.

After pool week, we made the drive to North Carolina for ocean rescue training, or surf training. I learned about reading currents and bringing a victim in from the surf. After surf training, we spent several days with the Coast Guard. The water on base was black as night. It had a dark red tint to it, and I'm not sure why. That was where we would do our night swims. There were stories floating around about agents freaking out during the night swims. Swimming at night "separates the men from the boys." Kelly and I just chuckled and whispered "I'm a lady" to each other when the instructors used those kinds of phrases.

On the night of our long night swim, we gathered at the dock around ten p.m. We strapped glow sticks and little lights to our snorkels so the instructors and boat drivers could do quick head counts. We hopped on the boat, and the driver sped away.

"Do not lose your swim buddy for any reason! See you where we started. First group, *go!*" One group at a time, we were told to get out of the boat and start swimming.

The current wasn't very strong, but there was enough movement to mandate some adjustments during the swim. Because of the darkness and the black water, I couldn't see my hands as I pulled with each stroke. It was a weird but thrilling experience. Every day in this course, I was proving to myself that I could, in fact, do hard things.

The next day was the one I was most excited about. It was time for my first helicopter jump. My ankles were throbbing by that point from wearing the long fins for hours upon hours. I realized being a collegiate swimmer meant little in this course. Being able to do a flip turn and follow a black line at the bottom of the pool only guaranteed my ability to swim fast.

We stood anxiously in the boat the next morning as the helicopter took off and flew over us. When it was Sean's and my turn, we jumped out of the boat and swam to the proper position. We were hauled up into the helicopter via the strop and waited. When the flight mechanic motioned to me, my heart leaped into my chest. I wasn't nervous until that moment. I was about to jump out of a perfectly good helicopter. I scooted until my legs and giant fins hung over the open doorway. I grabbed the bar to my left and waited for our carefully rehearsed sequence of events prior to jumping. With gear squared away, I waited for the last three slaps on my back, a signal that came way too quickly. Time to jump, swimmer.

I looked left. I looked right. I checked center. All clear. I thrust myself off the deck with my hands, kicked my feet straight ahead, grabbed my vest with my left hand, my mask with my right, and focused on the horizon. It was so loud on the way down until the thud of the splash silenced everything. I surfaced back to the roaring noise, gave the "I'm okay" signal, and swam out of the rotor wash that stung my face. No one could tell because of the snorkel, but I was smiling the biggest smile I'd ever smiled.

I actually had it in me to pass the course. I thanked my tired yet resilient body for holding on a little longer. To many in the military or elite training programs, jumping out of a helicopter is nothing noteworthy. To the girl from the High Desert with a long history of self-neglect and insecurity, that moment was incredibly special.

The last week of swim school was swift-water training, learning how to do water safety advances, and all the final exams. Swift-water training taught us how to swim in rapids and make rescues while doing it. We swam down a man-made flume, and each day the water level was different, which changed the rapids and flow dramatically. This part of the training was fun but painful. And the water was warm… and there were snakes in it.

I hate snakes. I grew up in the desert. Most snakes I saw had rattles, and I stayed far away from them. These, we were told, were harmless. I tried really hard to *not* jump out of my skin when I would see a little snake head pop up while we were training. One of the instructors heard me say something about disliking snakes and caught one of them. Like a child, he came up to me and the main WetMed instructor when we were practicing some medical scenarios. He shoved the snake toward me, and I about peed myself.

Swift-water training wasn't easy because rapids are dangerous. We practiced going feet first and headfirst down the flume and then added the rescues. During one headfirst swim, I whacked my knee on a rock. At the end of the run, we had to get out and walk back up to the top since the water was going too fast to swim upstream. We wore pants, shirts, and big boots for this training, so I couldn't look at it without taking my pants off, which is generally frowned upon in public. The lead instructor noticed my limp and asked if I was okay.

"This is the last week of class. I'll chop this leg off before I drop out now."

He chuckled and said, "Yeah, I've figured that out about you."

My knee was badly swollen by the end of the day, but aside from some really bad bruising and swelling and one decent gash, I was fine.

During our final week, we learned about rescue swimmer protection advances. They are more than just showing up in a wetsuit with a gun and gear. They involve water analysis (currents, temperature, depth, et cetera), ingress and egress points, emergency and alternative egress points along the route, as well as a multitude of other considerations to plan for in a water environment. Not to mention bodies of water often have line-of-sight issues, meaning it's hard to shield the protectee from every high point (i.e. potential sniper location). There are many countermeasures to implement in that type of situation. Unfortunately, I would not get the chance to do a presidential- or vice presidential-level water safety advance in my career, but I loved learning about them.

On the day of the final exams, I was nervous but weirdly calm. We were told our WetMed was going to be evaluated and scored by Johns Hopkins physicians who were on site for the day. If they said our WetMed wasn't sufficient, we would not pass. During my scenario, my victim—a plastic dummy—had a bleeder or a fast arterial bleed that needed to be addressed very quickly. I couldn't get to the bleed because of all the victim's clothes, so I took my scissors out of my vest and started to cut, but the scissors weren't doing the job quickly enough. I ditched the scissors and started to tear the fabric by hand. I got the job done, but I felt like I took too long. A rapidly bleeding victim didn't have time for mishaps. I was sure the Johns Hopkins doctors would deem that scenario unsatisfactory.

Waiting for my results was excruciating because we had to wait in the locker rooms. Since Kelly and I were the only two females, we were left to our dramatic devices while the guys were in the men's locker room.

"I did okay on the rescues and the swimming part. But those doctors had poker faces. I'm sure I failed," I said. Oh, gosh. Dramatic much?

An instructor knocked on the locker room door and called my name. I joined Sean, and we were led down a hallway with one of the doctors in tow. He looked at me and shook his head. Inside I died, and I knew he could tell because he instantly changed his tune and waved his hands as if to say, "No, no, no, you're fine. Don't worry." He was teasing me, but the poor guy didn't realize how much it meant to me.

I almost started crying when the lead instructor told me I'd passed. I, Melanie Lentz, had just become a US Secret Service Rescue Swimmer.

CHAPTER 13

CHOICES

STEVE PICKED ME UP FROM the airport, and I retold all the stories I'd been telling him and texting him about during the course. I couldn't help it. We'd been given our class photos when we graduated along with a photo of someone doing a helicopter jump. That someone was me. The lead instructor said, "Well guys, usually we hand out the same picture of someone jumping because we can't tell anyone apart with all the gear. You'd never know the difference. But the best jump picture was Lentz, so you'll just have to get past the blond ponytail." A couple of weeks after graduation, I heard that photo had been blown up and was hanging at headquarters.

Getting back to the office was anticlimactic. My direct supervisor hadn't checked on me one single time during the whole course. It's not that I had needed the validation or the checkup, but it was irritating that most of the other agents in the class were getting calls from their respective supervisors regularly just to see how they were doing. In hindsight, I needed to celebrate my own victories and not let anyone be a wet blanket on my accomplishment.

In the midst of all the campaign travel and swimming, 2012 was a memorable year. The more I was physically away from Steve, the more emotionally distant we seemed to become. It felt like I was the one calling him rather than him initiating texts or contact with me. Maybe he assumed I would call when I could since I was working out of town. But he began to take longer to answer texts and longer to answer calls than normal. The calls we had appeared to be more rushed.

Being in new cities and meeting new agents gave me plenty of opportunities to chat about Steve. I worked a Paul Ryan rally in Virginia, and the local lead advance was into old cars, so we talked about Steve's off-roading projects between paperwork and site visits.

"He seems like an awesome guy," he said once.

"He is," I said, and I knew it was true. Once in a while he'd do something that would make me realize why I stayed. We would slyly buy a couple's dinner at a restaurant and watch them look around wondering who had done it, smiling mischievously as we left the restaurant. I loved the kindness and generosity he was so quick to express to others. However—and I felt selfish and high-maintenance to admit it—very few of those kind moments appeared to be directed at me anymore.

I confided in my two best girlfriends Brit and Adisa about my frustrations. Adisa had an inkling about the unhappiness already. Not long before I told her, Steve and I were supposed to have a fun night out at the Laugh Factory with her and her husband. Steve decided not to come at the last minute, and I was really hurt because we rarely had a night out together with my friends. Most of our fun was spent with his friends.

Over coffee, I told Brit, "I don't know if I can stay married to Steve if something doesn't change."

I made a list of notes about my marriage on a random piece of lined paper sometime in 2012. I wrote a list of things I loved about Steve, things I loved about our marriage, things I wanted in a marriage, and what was lacking in my marriage. I wrote something at the bottom of the page that would resonate with me later when I reread it. It was written in 2012, but it may as well have been written at any point after 2008.

I wrote, *"I'm afraid that nothing will change unless something drastic happens. I'm afraid that if we separate, Steve will go back to his family, and I will be made into an enemy. My marriage would be over if he were forced to leave. If I am going to be required to take care of myself, I don't want someone else taking advantage of me. I'm afraid this is as good as it's gonna get, and I need to realize things won't go back to the way it was [sic] five years ago. We've changed, and that's that."*

I didn't expect Brit or Adisa to have all the answers, but I shocked myself when I verbally voiced my real feelings. It was a relief. Was I in the wrong to feel unhappy? I secretly prayed for the day when I would text him on my way home from work and he would respond, "Drive safe. Don't worry about dinner tonight. I've got it covered. Just get home." Was I wrong to want to feel more like spouses than roommates?

Our sex life may as well have been nonexistent. Of course, I was traveling a lot in 2012, but I did try to make an effort to keep things interesting. I always wanted Steve to know I was thinking about him when I was away. On three separate occasions, I sent Steve a naughty photo while we were apart. None of them were raunchy or anything. All were taken during moments when I was not thinking about some random fat pooch or lacking thigh gap. He never acknowledged any of them. When I asked if he'd gotten them, he just said, "You shouldn't be sending those kinds of pictures. I deleted it as soon as you sent it." I couldn't win.

As I've said, memories are often skewed in our favor. We remember what we want to remember when we're hurting. I know Steve put up with a lot that year. Maybe I never gave him enough credit for what he did. However, my truth and viewpoint at the time was that I married someone who had stopped seeing me and stopped caring about my happiness. That much I believed wholeheartedly in 2012.

I knew I had some choices to make. I researched annulments and divorce. I didn't think I would ever find myself looking at forms and requirements for ending my marriage. But I did. I learned that in California, an annulment needed to happen within the first five years of marriage. We were well within that timeline, and we didn't have any kids and met the other criteria. Paperwork-wise, ending things could potentially be easy. I kept it in the back of my mind, but I felt incredibly guilty for it. I wondered if he had done any research himself.

Shortly after my annulment research, journaling, and confessions to friends, I thought maybe I was rushing into things. After all, Steve and I had been together for five years and only married for two. We were just in a rough patch. I was not a quitter, and an annulment seemed like a quitter-esque move.

I made a choice at the end of 2012: I was staying with Steve. I didn't want anyone else. I wanted us to be happy, and I was going to do everything in my power to make things better between us.

Part of that choice involved a look at my career. I'd just accomplished a really big goal by passing the Rescue Swimmer course. What other goals did I have? Could I be content with what I had accomplished and once and for all put a big protection detail in DC out of my mind? Better yet, could I see myself doing something else with my life if staying in Los Angeles wound up not being an option?

I didn't have a lot of my answers then, but I made sure my career preferences showed the Reagan Protective Division (Nancy Reagan's detail) in Los Angeles at the top of my list. I had to be at peace with that, so I told myself it was best for my marriage. I figured the more I voiced it, the more it would be true. As far as anyone in the office knew, I wanted to stay in Los Angeles as long as my career would let me.

Once the campaign was over and work had settled down, I

suggested that Steve and I figure out something to do together, just the two of us. We always had fun when we got away from the everyday humdrum of our lives. He took me waterskiing with his dad a couple of times, and I absolutely loved it! It seemed like most of our adventures revolved around off-roading with his friends, and I missed our adventures together.

I found a half-marathon series in wine country in northern California. Steve had previously mentioned that he wanted to visit that part of the state. So what better excuse to go three times in 2013 than a half-marathon series? Steve didn't want to run with me, but he thought it would be fun to take the trips, so I booked everything and started training.

I had a great time on those trips in 2013. I realized how much I had missed Steve. I missed us. We kayaked the day after the first race in the series. It made me think of Savannah when we went kayaking and talked on the park bench for hours. We drove through all the vineyards, trying to find the Polesky-Lentz vineyard after another race because I wanted a picture standing next to a vineyard with the name Lentz in it. We never found it, but Steve was always a fan of road trips and didn't mind cruising around.

To top it off, during that time, Steve got hired as the School Resource Officer at the same police department where he'd been a reserve officer. It wasn't a full-time position, but it was something he enjoyed. He coached high school wrestling while we were in college, so being around high schoolers was a good fit for him. The school loved him, and even though there were a lot of troubled kids there, he won their trust. I loved hearing about his workdays and how he was trying to make a positive influence in the lives of the students.

Steve asked me to come by the school one day, and he introduced me to some of the teachers who gushed about how much they loved him. Class let out when we were walking, and I saw him greet some of the students by name. Many of the high school girls had googly eyes for Steve. I thought their little

..e cute. "I can't blame them," I told him. But I ..oned him to be careful.

I don't know why I had felt the need to say it. I just knew how likable and approachable he was. I didn't want him to give a boy-crazy, impressionable high school girl the wrong idea by being too kind. I wasn't jealous or threatened by those girls, but Steve seemed to think I was being a paranoid wife. I just thought I was looking out for him.

Since I'd committed to trying to stay in Los Angeles by getting on the list for the Nancy Reagan detail, we decided to plant roots in the San Gabriel Valley and buy a house. In March 2013, at age twenty-eight, I bought our first house. I loved that little house! In the same month, my parents moved to the Midwest and my sister to Utah, leaving me with no immediate family nearby. I was not close with Steve's family, something that continually to bother me. For the first time in my adult life, I didn't have my parents and sister close by.

I was still in the Protective Intelligence (PI) squad, and I'd gotten better at working the cases and used to dealing with headquarters and the supervisory micromanagement of cases. I needed to trust my instincts and not act wishy-washy about threat cases. It's easy to be noncommittal in reports because you're afraid if you're wrong it will come back and bite you. Choices and recommendations had to be made, so I couldn't lack assertiveness, something I seemed to struggle with from time to time.

My confidence and judgment were put to the test on June 7, 2013. I was assigned a PI advance for President Obama's visit to Peter Chernin's house in Santa Monica for a fund-raiser. I was partnered with an agent from Headquarters' Protective Intelligence Division (PID) for the visit, and we worked with local law enforcement throughout the advance and the visit. That way, all basic communication bases were covered... in theory.

The advance went smoothly for the most part. There were a

few tips that came in, and we worked them out, but other than a planned demonstration near the home in Santa Monica, there wasn't a lot of significant intelligence-related traffic.

When we arrived at the Chernin residence with the president, the PID counterpart went inside. I stayed outside with a Santa Monica police officer to monitor the demonstrations and any other potential hazards.

It wasn't long before the radios and Blackberrys started chirping with traffic about an active shooter at Santa Monica College, just a few miles from our location. I'd never been in a situation like that. There was so much radio traffic and information flooding radios and inboxes like a fire hose, much of which wound up being incorrect, but it was the best information available at the time.

By that time, the Regional Call Center at the Los Angeles Field Office—basically a command post or dispatch center we called the Duty Desk—was sending out messages to us when all the chaos started. I found this interesting since the actual intelligence advance agents (me and the PID counterpart) were on the ground getting different information.

The police officer with me was amazing. He relayed in real time what was coming out over the radio, and I passed along what I got to our team and the Duty Desk as quickly as possible. One big thing I wanted to keep track of was how large the search perimeter was getting around the school. We were close but not right next to the college. But the wider the search perimeter got, the more likely it was to interfere with our motorcade routes.

In the midst of all that, the planned demonstration had grown quite large (several hundred) and was starting to get rowdy. There was some chatter among the demonstrators about taking over an intersection a few blocks away from our secure area, but it was a potential egress for the motorcade at that point. A PI agent in the area called me.

"Hey, Mel," he said. "I wanted to let you know that the Duty Desk just told me to leave and go to the college's command post that's being set up right now. They want me to monitor the shooting activity from there."

I was pissed. I didn't care who gave that order. It was not happening.

"Listen to me," I responded confidently. "You're monitoring a demonstration of hundreds of people with a direction of interest toward our protectee. They haven't been through magnetometers, and they're talking about blocking the intersection. If we have to go that way to get out of here due to barricades associated with this unrelated shooting, it could be a problem. As far as we know, this shooting has nothing to do with our protectee right now. Do not leave your post. If anyone gives you crap about that, you tell that person to call me. I'll let them know they have no right to make that call from where they're sitting in their comfy chair."

"I totally agree with you."

"Thanks. Keep me posted. If something changes here, I'll let you know." With that we hung up. Someone else in the office would need to go to the college's command post. We had our own PI issues that needed immediate attention. I wondered for a millisecond if I was going to get reprimanded at the debriefing.

Law enforcement as well as the general public always have a million trains of thought and a million scenarios to "what if…" someone's split-second choices. But no matter how many ways this scenario is spun, the fact remains that shortly after telling the PI agent to stay put, several demonstrators blocked the intersection and were arrested. The college shooter, John Zawahri, killed several people and was killed by police at the college. President Obama's route was unhindered after some adjustments, and everyone on our end went home safe. I know my decision was not wrong, and I'll stand by it. It was one of the first times I'd ever stood up to a supervisor or a senior agent. Tactically, I was inexperienced, and I typically let those with more experience lead situations outside my expertise. Even though we'd been trained at the same academy, experience does matter. In this situation, I didn't have the luxury of defaulting to someone more experienced.

I didn't press the issue at the debriefing, and no one challenged my decision, even at the management level. Surely if I could keep my wits about me in that kind of situation and take appropriate and confident action when needed, then I could certainly demonstrate sound judgment in my personal life… right?

CHAPTER 14

REALITY CHECKS

S TEVE AND I BECAME PROFESSIONALS at getting along. I don't say that as a humble brag. We had a knack for avoiding tough conversations as well as the big issues between us. That philosophy, apparently, was how I had resolved to make things better: ignore the issues. Steve worked regular school hours during the week, and if I wasn't traveling or working in-town protection, I worked a standard nine-to-five schedule. Therefore, we had more evenings and weekends together for the first time in years.

Our days usually consisted of my waking up around four a.m. to exercise before work. Leaving early helped me avoid the worst of the LA traffic at least one way. Usually, once per week my friend Brit and I ran the Hill at LAPD's academy before work, and I swam a few of the other mornings with a couple of other friends. I got home later than Steve because of the evening commute. After I got home, I would make dinner and pack lunches for the next day, probably start a load of laundry, and then we'd shower together.

Showering together was rarely sexual though. It was mostly just time to talk about random stuff. Steve was still building off-roading rigs, so sometimes he would say something like, "So do you want to learn the difference between a Dana 60 and a Dana 40 today or should I teach you how a drive shaft works? Hey, pass the soap." Random shower talk.

After showers, we usually binge-watched some TV shows until I couldn't keep my eyes open anymore. Then we'd go to bed, and I'd be asleep in two minutes or less. That daily life scenario was not miserable on the surface. For good chunks of time, it seemed like we actually liked each other. I felt like I'd made the right decision to keep trying.

On Christmas Day 2013, I had a rare major holiday off. Steve worked a patrol shift since school was out. He was supposed to get off at five, and then we'd meet at his mom's house for dinner with his extended family. But a little after five, he called me.

"Mel, I'm going to be late. I just had a really bad call. A toddler drowned in her family pool, and I was first on the scene."

Steve had responded to a lot of difficult situations during patrol shifts — teen suicides, domestic violence, et cetera — but he always seemed to handle himself and recover from it. He'd talk about it briefly in little factoids as if he was reciting his police report, and then that would be the end of it.

We watched a lot of Grey's Anatomy together. We called it Steve's "stories" like my great-grandparents referred to their daily soap operas as stories. For a few weeks, whenever the long beeping sound of a person flatlining in the hospital came on the show, Steve would say something like, "That sound makes me think about that little girl on the table at the hospital. I can still see her."

In the midst of those sad yet communicative moments, we seemed to be okay. We were comfortable. Familiar. In an unpredictable work life, we were something — often the only thing—consistent and constant. Sometimes it was easier not to discuss anything too controversial about the two of us because our problems often seemed minuscule compared to the tragedies and difficulties in our jobs. Our jobs made us good at defusion rather than resolution. Police respond to difficult calls on a regular basis. It's easier to defuse the situation by arresting the offender. The judicial system or social services could sort out the resolution. Unfortunately, defusion in a marriage leads nowhere positive, but it certainly is sustainable for a while.

It was around that time, though, that I was told some of Steve's family had made unkind statements about me when I wasn't around. Steve's mom and I had a spat at one point before that, and I didn't do myself any favors in the way I reacted. My heart was in the right place, but I inserted myself into a family matter when it wasn't my place. I thought we had worked things out. I apologized, but she and I remained a passive state of awkward.

"Mel, I don't understand how you can expect me to pick between you and my family. It's like you want me to make that choice, and it's not fair," he said when I had told him it seemed like he didn't have my back when it came to his family.

But I really just wanted him to act like he and I were a team, that we were each other's top priority. We had families, of course, but I wanted us to be our own family unit too. I was faced with a tough question: How long do I keep trying to have relationships with people who don't want a close relationship with me? It was a sad reality check the day I decided to remove any expectation of a close relationship with Steve's family. I would always try to be kind, but I'd understand my place on the outskirts of the family's inner circle.

Deep down, I blamed Steve and made myself the victim. It was easier that way.

Sometime between 2013 and 2014, my work phone rang.

"Hey, Melanie. Dave and John here from Water Safety." It was the two main instructors from rescue swimmer school.

"We've been talking over here. We heard you were trying to stay in Los Angeles to go to RPD [Reagan Protective Division] or BPD [George H. W. Bush Protective Division]. We don't want to overstep, but we really think you would excel here in DC. Seriously. I guess we're trying to talk you out of it."

I started choking up. *Please don't do this, guys.*

"We watched the latest HAMMER class come through, and we think you'd definitely be able to pass if that's something you're interested in."

HAMMER, or Hazardous Agent Mitigation Medical Response, is a special group of agents trained to respond in the event of an environmental emergency such as the introduction of a hazardous chemical agent near the protectee. HAMMER agents are all trained as emergency medical technicians, and they go through a rigorous and difficult training course. At the time, only a few women had passed the course.

They had no idea what was going on in my personal life or the reasons for my career decisions after passing rescue swimmer school. I'm pretty sure I told them that trying to get on RPD or BPD (which was in Houston, Texas, but had some options for Steve in terms of easier out-of-state police transfers) was the best thing for my personal life because my husband was a local police officer. I don't know if I went any deeper and told them things weren't great at home because I was delusional about the status of my marriage most of the time. I know I thanked them, and when I hung up, I put my head in my hands at my desk and tried to reason with myself.

Am I doing the right thing? Yes, yes, I am. I'm fine with this. But I do well with the medical stuff. I'd love to be an EMT. They don't understand. Every marriage involves compromise and sacrifice. This is mine. I've already decided. Why am I second-guessing now?

Because I'm not happy.

I also got a call from an agent on BPD. He said some rescue swimmers were due to transfer off the detail soon and they were looking to replace them. He said he thought I'd love the detail and should consider throwing my name into the mix. Being a rescue swimmer might bump me to the top of the list, he said.

That appealed to me a lot. I knew a couple of people on that detail, and I'd always heard good things about morale there. I had broached the subject with Steve against my better judgment. It resulted in a fight where I unfairly and angrily said, "I'm putting my name in for Houston. You can come with me or you cannot." As agency politics go, I was not selected, and a nonrescue swimmer with five years' seniority on me got the spot. It wound up being a nonissue. Ah, but it was an issue.

In April 2014, I transferred out of the Protective Intelligence squad and into the Protection Operations (Pro Ops) squad in the Los Angeles Field Office. I was happy about this change. The Assistant to the Special Agent in Charge (ATSAIC) of this squad at the time was my favorite boss. The office maintained a list of squad preferences as well as protection detail preferences. I had put Pro Ops on my preferences mostly because of the boss but also because it was a purely protection squad. I preferred protection to investigations any day of the week.

Pro Ops was in charge of protection logistics in the Los Angeles Field Office. It was a small squad, and we coordinated in-town protection visits and maintained the ROTA, the travel rotation within the office. For example, if DC got notice that a foreign head of state was coming to Los Angeles, they'd call us, and we'd get local personnel assigned to coordinate the protection aspects of the visit. In addition, if Pro Ops in DC called and said they needed ten Los Angeles agents to travel to Las Vegas for an Obama fund-raiser, the Pro Ops squad would be in charge of selecting and notifying ten agents from the current ROTA for the assignment. The bosses in the office nicknamed Pro Ops "the Body Snatchers."

Soon after I transferred to Pro Ops, I was told to start going over the paperwork for Operation Companion, which was the demise plan for former First Lady Nancy Reagan. I was to take over as the lead advance for the operation because the current lead was transferring to DC. When a protectee dies, they're protected until they're laid to rest. So, if Mrs. Reagan passed away, I would be in charge of coordinating the movements from the house to the funeral home, et cetera.

This plan was not new. Nancy Reagan was in her nineties by then and in reasonably good health. Operation Companion had been updated and discussed regularly as needed for years. The advance team was preassigned. The paperwork and notification emails were already drafted. There was a list of tasks to be done in a specific order once Mrs. Reagan passed away.

As I transitioned into the lead position, I toured the funeral home with the site agent, met with the staff there, saw the rooms where she would be held, and reviewed the routes. There was a contingency plan for everything. It was a little morbid, but it was something that required preplanning.

By 2014, agency morale was very low. Los Angeles Field Office morale was no exception. Agents were leaving for other government or private sector jobs. Scandals and more scandals resulted in further morale decline. Due to the increased attrition, agents were on the ROTA more often and traveling way more than they had before. Therefore, the attitudes declined and agents became disgruntled and difficult to work with. In other words, the Body Snatchers were not an office favorite.

But I loved the work even though I was working longer hours in the office than I ever had before. Pro Ops made me feel like I had tasks or problems I could solve. The work felt meaningful, and I really liked everyone in my squad. They were all hard workers who weren't afraid to put in the figurative elbow grease to get the job done.

A couple of months after transferring to Pro Ops, there was chatter about transfers coming for Mrs. Reagan's protection detail. The office supervisors confirmed I still wanted to go there, and it looked like I was near the top of the list. It was really just a big tease because nothing actually happened except every couple of months I was told that transfers were pending and expected very soon.

But the happiest part of 2014 was Steve's getting hired as a full-time police officer. I gushed and cried when he told me it was official. He would remain the School Resource Officer for the remainder of the school year and then transition to full-time patrol.

"I'm so proud of you, Steve!" *Look at him! He's so happy. He's officially a full-time police officer. He's finally landed his dream job. Maybe now he'll see me. Maybe now we can be a family and a team.*

But the arguments continued. We'd agreed to wait until we were thirty to talk about starting a family, and we both had turned thirty in 2014. I wasn't sure I could be the mother I wanted to be if I remained an agent. This is not a criticism of the wonderful and loving mothers who are also Secret Service agents. I applaud them for being able to make it work. I guess I didn't want to try to balance motherhood and the chaos of being an agent. I wanted the opportunity to pursue something else, and I couldn't do that if Steve wasn't reliable and consistent. This was never new news to Steve. Yet it was still a source of contention over the years.

"Mel, it's like you're giving me an ultimatum. Get a job or we're not having kids. I hate ultimatums."

"Steve, we've been over and over this. It's not an ultimatum. It's about being responsible with bringing a new life into this world."

"Well, you know what? Every time we talk about this, the circumstances aren't perfect. They're never going to be perfect. It's like you're okay with not having kids at all."

"Oh, for goodness' sake, Steve. You care more about being a father than you do about being a husband."

"I've always known I wanted to be a dad, Mel."

"I know. I'm scared. You think I'm happy with how things have played out here?" *I want us to be okay more than anything in this world.*

We eventually had a rational conversation for once about family planning once he was hired full time. If I got onto the Reagan detail, the dangling carrot in my career, it would be a good time to get pregnant. Since Mrs. Reagan didn't travel much anymore, it was possible to work at her residence in the command post while on light duty as a pregnant agent. The tentative plan was to get on the Reagan detail and try to get pregnant. I had so much sick leave and accrued vacation time that I'd have plenty of leave to use after the baby was born. After that, I would leave the Secret Service and pursue another line of work if I couldn't balance a child and the job.

But the Reagan transfer didn't come and didn't come. I didn't travel a lot in Pro Ops, and I missed traveling. Steve was promptly assigned to the graveyard shift as soon as the school year was over. We had opposite schedules and often went days without seeing each other due to my long commutes and his overnight shifts. It was sad that I could go home to the house I loved, see that my husband had been there and slept in our bed during the day but not physically see him. I'd shower alone while his towel hung on the rod, still damp from his shower a couple of hours prior.

Around the summer of 2014, Steve got into a fight with a large mentally ill man while he was on patrol. Steve was tall and lean. We joked that he had "blegs," a term coined by a college friend, because it was hard to tell where his legs ended and his butt began. But Steve could handle himself due to all his previous wrestling and martial arts training. He was okay, thank God.

That incident was a big reality check for me as a female agent. I was in great shape athletically and prided myself on maintaining a high level of fitness. But if I had to fight that guy, I would probably be dead unless I could have unholstered my gun in time. That was the reality. The other reality was that I had interviewed countless mentally ill subjects in my PI investigations, many who were much larger than me. Any number of them could have attacked me without warning.

Those are the dangers of the job, and I was vastly unprepared.

I had lead courage. I took being armed for granted. I made the assumption that I could get to my gun if I needed to. I made the assumption that my sidearm would give me the power to neutralize a bad situation. How utterly wrong I was, and Steve's incident opened my eyes.

The Secret Service is obsessively focused on image. Supervisors would refer to agents as squared away if they looked good in a suit and had to get them tailored to accommodate their bulging biceps and small waists. Many agents were given prominent assignments if they looked the part. Being able to run fast and bench press a crazy amount of weight implied an agent was an adequate defense against all foes, foreign and domestic. I subscribed to the line of thought that a fit agent is a disciplined agent who was likely to respond more appropriately than a slug agent in a suit who eats donuts all day. But come on, fitness is something, but protection is not all about fitness.

But what if I can't get to my gun in time? What if the attacker takes me down? I haven't done any sort or fighting, sparring, or control tactics since Beltsville. There's something seriously wrong with that.

The day after Steve's fight, I started researching martial arts studios and gyms near the Los Angeles Field Office. No one was going to say I was a worthless female agent if I ever had to actually fight someone.

In July 2014, I joined a Krav Maga studio in Downtown Los Angeles. It was very humbling to walk in and start from scratch in the beginner classes like every new member who came through the door. I hadn't thrown a punch since Beltsville, and that was really unacceptable. I hadn't forgotten all my training, but learning how to defend myself without the gun was an eye opener. I simply hadn't practiced, and neither had most of the agents I worked with every day.

I became a little obsessed with Krav Maga. It would wind up being my escape from life soon enough. Getting my butt kicked every day might seem a bit masochistic, but to me those bruises and practice made me a better agent.

CHAPTER 15

THE LAST
ANNIVERSARY

MORALE WITHIN THE LOS ANGELES Field Office was starting to wear on me by 2015. Everyone seemed to be pissed at the Protection Operations (Pro Ops) squad because we were snatching bodies from the investigative squads right and left for protection assignments. I hated the attitudes. Pro Ops never got a full day off. That's not an exaggeration. The cell phone went off for something one of us had to deal with every single day.

The supervisors in the other squads wouldn't give up their agents for trips until the last possible deadline. It happened so often that Pro Ops in DC started calling and asking why we didn't have our act together. Even when upper management would intervene, nothing changed. In the meantime, Pro Ops agents were staying late doing the paperwork we could have done earlier had they not been trying to prove a point. What was their point? I suspect it went something to the tune of "My guys are overworked and need a break." Join the club, I wanted to tell them.

But it was true. Everyone across the board was growing increasingly tired and run-down. I couldn't change it from my desk in Pro Ops. I couldn't say, "Oh, never mind. Take the day off. I will let the visiting prime minister know we are too tired to protect him."

Steve and I remained on different schedules. He worked weekend graveyard shifts while I remained on weekday day shifts unless something came up for protection. Since he was a new full-time officer, vacation time needed to be accrued. Therefore, our weekends weren't free to spend time together. Instead, I tried to get out of the house so he could sleep. We saw each other, but it was usually briefly. When he was off during the week, he usually went to his dad's to work on his truck while I was working.

A group of officers, cadets, and dispatchers at Steve's police department went on off-roading adventures usually once or twice each month. He asked me if I wanted to go with them sometimes. I did want to go, but Pro Ops was busy all the time. It seemed like the days they were going were always when a presidential visit was in town or when someone else in the squad was on leave. Pro Ops only had a handful of agents and had to work around each other's requested leave. I felt bad for even asking for the time off because of how consistently swamped we were. Plus they always went off-roading on weekdays because many cops have their regular days off on weekdays. As usual, I couldn't win.

In other words, I said "yes" to work more often than I made an effort to take time off for my husband. Over time, Steve started talking about all these awesome coworkers like they were the greatest people in the world. He had so much fun with them and seemed to prefer their company. In hindsight, we were both probably going where we felt most validated… him to work, his family, and his off-roading friends while I went to work where my friends were and the Krav Maga gym where I didn't have to talk about work or my marriage. It spelled toxicity without much forethought, but my dysfunctional love for Steve was overshadowed by an unhealthy attachment. Familiarity can be comforting if contorted enough to mask the toxic parts.

Steve bought mountain bikes, something he'd been talking about doing for a while. The San Gabriel Valley foothills have many great trails for hiking and mountain biking. In an effort to make time for us to spend together doing something fun—just the two of us—I had suggested that maybe we needed to have a date night once per week. Steve didn't initiate these kinds of things, and as usual, I resented him for it. But we settled on Tuesday nights. I would make every effort to get off work early every Tuesday, a day he was also typically off work.

We went on a couple of mountain-biking date nights. The first time, we rode on the trails near our house and then rode to an awesome little Mexican place for dinner. Another time we rode to the cute little downtown area where we lived and had dinner. We saw a tarantula on one of the trails. I was tentative on the trails, but Steve was so agile and good at riding through them quickly. I was much slower, and despite my complaining ("Slow down, I'm going to break my neck!"), we needed that time together.

I reminded him on Tuesday mornings that it was date night when I left for work. After a couple of weeks, I genuinely forgot to remind him on my way out the door. But I knew it was Tuesday, and when I got home, he wasn't there.

I texted him and said something like, "Hey, I'm home. Where are you?"

A few minutes later he responded that he was working on his truck with his dad.

"Will you be a while?"

"Yeah, probably. We're right in the middle of something."

He had forgotten about date night.

I don't remember if I mentioned it to him or not, but it hurt my feelings that our date night wasn't a priority to him or something worth remembering. Was he expecting me to remind him every week? But then in the next minute, I thought maybe it was an innocent mistake. Sometimes people forget. I could understand that. I wasn't perfect at remembering everything. I let it go the first time, but then it happened again the next week and the week after. One week he was hanging out with his new coworker off-road friends. Date nights just stopped happening.

I still came home early every Tuesday, hoping and wishing for him to be there with a smile on his face, saying "Hey, babe, you ready to go on a date?" I used it as yet another reason to make him the bad guy.

I was jealous of his new off-roading friends because they were getting the passionate, fun Steve I had fallen in love with. I was so tired of feeling like second fiddle to his affection. I lashed out at him sometimes about it and then went back to packing his lunches and making his dinners and all the other things I did every day that he rarely acknowledged. Bitterness was probably oozing from my pores.

The topic of sex came up in arguments sometimes. I asked for us to make an effort to be more intimate. One time he said, "I would be fine with not having sex." The amount of hurt I felt in that moment brought me to a new low. The most hurtful statements are often the most honest. Was he getting it somewhere else? If not me, then whom? I'd been around too many guys at work, and I heard them talk about their sexual conquests.

I told Steve how much his statement bothered me, and he minimized it by saying, "You're taking what I said out of context." He didn't tell me he was attracted to me. He didn't apologize.

I took that statement very hard, obviously. Why would he want to be intimate with his blubbering, crying, depressed workaholic of a wife? *I've officially lost my charm,* I thought. *No wonder he isn't here. I don't even like myself very much right now. Who can blame him?*

Our anniversary was in April. Our anniversaries were never lavish. We never did more than maybe go out to dinner. But that year I wanted to go to a hotel on our anniversary night. Maybe it was subconsciously a last-ditch effort to connect with him.

I'd worked with a lovely lady at a fancy hotel in Pasadena, California, during a semirecent protectee's visit. She'd sent me an email saying April was Government Employee Appreciation Month, and they were offering discounted rates for anyone interested in staying with them. I asked her about staying on our anniversary. She helped me set up a room after Steve agreed to go. He didn't say, "Oh, yeah. We definitely need that. What a fun spontaneous idea, Mel. You're not such a wet blanket after all." He just said, "Yeah, okay."

"Did you have anything else planned or in mind?"

"No," he replied.

You seem superexcited, I thought sarcastically.

The hotel had a really nice steakhouse. I made a reservation there too, because Steve liked steak. I didn't like steak, but I could always get something else. I thought it would be a fun little getaway even if it was just a twenty-minute drive from home.

The hotel contact went out of her way to make our stay beautiful. She had chocolate-covered strawberries sent to the room, special touches and extras sent from the chef at dinner, and even had flowers for me at check-in. It felt so luxurious, so unlike anything I'd ever experienced before.

Steve kept making comments about having to dress nicely for dinner and how pompous the clientele was and how this just wasn't his scene. It wasn't my typical scene either. I'd never been part of this type of luxury except from the sidelines as dignitaries partook. We were experiencing something new and rare. Why couldn't he just appreciate it without the stupid comments? I was afraid someone would overhear him, especially when he made a comment about them bringing champagne to the table.

Steve never drank alcohol. I tried to make it a joke, taking a sip of my own glass and discreetly swapping glasses with him so it looked like he'd had a sip. I was smiling and trying to have fun, feeling grateful and overwhelmed by the hospitality and the beauty of the hotel. We wouldn't have been able to afford a place like that any other time.

My idea, of course, was to avoid our normal routine and just have some actual intimacy and enjoy each other's company. No distractions or dogs, just a beautiful hotel room, a comfy bed, and time together. What did Steve suggest? Ordering a movie in the room. What did we watch? *Hot Tub Time Machine II.* Not even the first one, but the sequel. By the end of the movie, I regretted ever trying to plan a nice anniversary. We slept and checked out the next morning, and I poorly disguised my hurt. What was happening to us?

Upper management in the field office continued to tease me with hints that I'd be transferred to Mrs. Reagan's protection detail, but no transfer orders came out. I was miserable at work, and I was ranting about it at home a lot, something I did too much of, I know. I'd get home and feel the need to release all the tension of the day, finally in a safe place to gripe about the jerks I'd dealt with all day. It turned into an almost daily thing. There was no escape, only long hours of work followed by a traffic-fueled Los Angeles commute home, followed by another miserable evening just to wake up feeling miserable the next day. I felt depressed and sad all the time. Somehow I stayed focused and present at work but was inwardly falling apart at the seams.

"I don't understand why you just can't be happy," Steve would say. I didn't even know what made me happy anymore. Steve and a meaningful job used to make me happy. Now both seemed to be doing just the opposite.

In May 2015, I went back to Beltsville for the rescue swimmer recertification, a one-week refresher all rescue swimmers were supposed to attend every so often. Since it had been three years since I'd gone through the course, I asked my boss to submit my name. He did, and I was selected. There were only four people who recertified that year, including a supervisor from the George H. W. Bush detail.

I did well at the recertification, and I had a blast as usual. I didn't know how difficult those recertifications were, so I had been training. The George H. W. Bush supervisor asked if I was interested in transferring to Houston to be on his detail. Bush wasn't boating as much as he used to, but they still needed rescue swimmers on the detail. *Oh no. Here we go again, I thought.* I'd been told by then that my Reagan Protective Division transfer was supposedly coming in August, but I'd yet to see anything official. I wasn't holding my breath. Also, now that Steve was working full time, I politely declined.

"My husband's job is in California. The Reagan detail is best for both of us."

The following month, Steve and I went to Colorado to visit his best friend and his family. I'd registered for a triathlon that weekend, and my parents flew in to watch the race.

When we were flying home, Steve and I started talking about Opel GTs, an old German car that looks like a mini Corvette. My mom had a 1973 Opel GT when she and my dad had gotten married. It was her baby. But when she had me—a real baby—she sold it, and my dad came home with a station wagon to replace it. Her sporty car wasn't car seat friendly. When I'd learned about her selling her dream car, I told her, "Mama, someday when I have a grown-up job, I'm going to buy you another Opel GT. I'm going to show up at your house in it, and it's going to have a giant bow on top. You just wait, Mama. I'm going to do it." I was in high school when I first said that.

Steve knew about my little promise to my mom, and we'd casually looked at Craigslist a couple of times without any luck. But that day, Steve found a red 1973 Opel GT not far from Los Angeles International Airport where we would be landing. It was in decent shape, meaning it wasn't a total pile of rust like most of the ones we'd seen online, but it needed a lot of work.

"Want to go look at it?" Steve asked.

"Do you think we can swing it if it's worth the money?"

"Can't hurt to go look." Steve called the seller, and we wound up buying the car that afternoon.

Buying that Opel GT was the last fun thing Steve and I did together. Steve loved working on cars, and he set about researching the vehicle and learning the ins and outs of it.

"This car is simple, Mel! I can totally work on this!" He was happy. We got online and made a detailed list of what needed to be done on the car. Well, Steve was online reading those items to me, and I was creating a list with prices and item numbers. Even though Steve complained that I hated off-roading and resented him for spending so much money on his truck, he truly didn't realize how much I enjoyed working on cars with him.

The night we made that list next to each other on the couch, it felt like 2007.

Soon after the Opel purchase, my official Reagan detail transfer orders came out. August 9, 2015, was my report date to the Reagan Protective Division. Finally. Steve was working full time, I was getting out of the Los Angeles Field Office and the bad morale, and I was going to work protection full time even if it was a very small detail.

I went to the gynecologist and talked to the doctor about going off birth control. There was a part of me that was still hesitant about having a baby, but everything seemed to be working out now. I knew the circumstances would never be perfect, like Steve had said. Maybe now was as good as it was going to get. We would get better now. It was all going to work out.

I kept an old empty birth control pack and bought Steve a birthday card. His birthday was at the beginning of August, right before my Reagan report date. My plan was to put the empty pack in his card. I calculated that my current pack was going to run out a few days after his birthday. Surely that would make him happy with me. I rehearsed my "Wanna have a baby?" speech in anticipation.

I was lighter on my feet in Pro Ops after that. The end was in sight. Since I had transfer orders, I was sent to the Reagan detail for a few temporary assignments so I could learn the ropes and get to know the members of the small detail, most of whom I already knew because they came from the LA office. I was even able to get a day off to go off-roading with Steve and his coworkers.

The off-roading trip was full of laughs and fun. We went to Big Bear and drove on the trails. But there was one thing: I sensed something was off. It was hard to pinpoint, but I'd sensed Steve and a female cadet were closer than he'd let on. We'd had a couple of discussions about her, and I admit to feeling a little jealous about the way he talked about her.

"Yeah, she's supercool. Her family is big into off-roading, and they vacationed where I used to as a kid. She's got her own Jeep. Well, her dad gave it to her, but she knows what she's doing on the trails and stuff."

Steve and I had our problems, yes, but we had an element of trust that needed to be there with all the time we spent apart. I admit to being insecure at times. I think that's probably a given at this point. But since he'd made the comment about being okay without sex, I'd begun to second-guess my intuition. He'd never given me a reason not to trust him, at least not one I had recognized.

He didn't hide the friendship with this cadet, but after seeing them interact, I suspected one or both felt something stronger than friendship. I didn't hate her for it if she did. It's not like she was the first girl to have a crush on my husband since we'd been together. But something was off. Maybe it was how charming he seemed to be acting around her. Maybe it was that she was genuinely interested in the off-roading and camping and I felt threatened because he'd accused me of hating both.

What happened was not necessarily her fault. I didn't say anything when we'd gotten home that night. I really hadn't wanted another fight. I wanted to make sure I wasn't wrong, but I couldn't think of a way to prove myself wrong except to talk to him about it. I'd decided to just let it go for that night, but I stewed about it all day at work the next day. The part that bothered me the most was how he'd acted with her. Charming. It seemed like all this girl was talking about was materialistic, superficial stuff. *Oh, for goodness' sake, little girl.* Steve seemed to be eating it all up, acting so impressed with her and looking at her when he was talking to the group.

Maybe I was legitimately overreacting, but I called Steve on my way home from work.

"Hey, I need to talk to you about something important when I get home… something that bothered me a lot." I said it calmly. I am sure of that. I wanted to communicate without a fight for once.

"Okay," was all he said.

I was more nervous about that conversation than anything in my life. I took a deep breath and told him that I had a weird feeling about him and Off-Road Cadet. I told him it seemed like they were closer than he'd let on. I didn't think I'd approached it in an accusatory way. In fact, I thought I'd deflected more toward her than him, implying that she was the one with feelings for him.

He reacted oddly. It's hard to explain. But had that scene been played out in a cheesy detective television show, the detective's response would have been "Are you sure that's the truth, or do you want to try again?"

"Oh my God, Mel. Are you serious? I haven't done anything wrong."

"I didn't say that. I said the way you two interacted bothered me, and I want to talk about it. Maybe it's as simple as this: she has a thing for you. In that case, you need to be careful how you interact with her. You might be giving her the wrong idea. If I were her, I might be getting the wrong idea."

"Mel, you've got it wrong. There's nothing going on. Why are you being jealous and paranoid?" *Because you acted like 2007 Steve with her.*

"Steve, I really don't want to fight with you. I've been trying to figure out how to talk about this without fighting. That's why I waited a whole day to bring it up. Please, Steve. Talk to me."

"What do you want me to say?"

"Steve, your wife… that's me… is saying she didn't like how you acted with a twenty-year-old yesterday. You need to understand this bothers me a lot. As my husband, you owe it to me to have an honest conversation where you don't minimize my feelings. What's going on with this girl? Something is going on, and maybe it's just her. After all, I can't blame her." I winked and smiled to lighten things up. *I'm really trying here, Steve.*

"Nothing is going on! You're reading into this. It's like you think I'm having an affair or something." He was getting agitated quickly. *He's going to shut down on me. Don't lose your temper, Mel. Keep it together. This is serious. Don't let him make you feel otherwise.*

"Why are you reacting this way? Does she have a thing for you?"

"I don't know. Maybe."

"Do you talk on the phone or hang out when I'm not around? I know she texts you sometimes." I'd known about some texts, not because I'd gone through his phone but because they'd popped up on his phone screen when we were together.

"Mel, nothing is going on. I don't know what to say to you to make you believe me."

"Let me see your phone then." It felt so weird to hear those words come out of my mouth. We both knew each other's phone passwords. I never went through his phone, and to my knowledge, he never went through mine.

He handed me his phone, and I proceeded to see six months of texts between this girl and my husband. The texts were not sexual, but some were a little flirtatious. Steve told me this girl had a boyfriend. If I were her boyfriend, I wouldn't have liked to have seen that quantity of texts with a married man. There were texts when I was out of town at the rescue swimmer recertification when we were in Colorado with my parents. It was pretty much a daily thing after a while. But I also noticed that he, not her, initiated most of the exchanges.

All attempts at keeping the peace went out the window. I was devastated, and I lost my temper, crying and screaming at him for betraying me that way.

"How could you? I'm right here, Steve! I'm going to Reagan's detail in just a couple of weeks. You're working full time and almost off your probationary period. We have a house and the dogs, and things were supposed to be looking up. I can't believe you would stoop this low. No wonder she felt so comfortable acting all chummy and flirty with you all day yesterday. You made it okay."

He'd accused me of being insecure, jealous, oversensitive, and just plain wrong. He'd minimized his actions, saying, "We only texted like once a day, Mel." He'd even admitted he liked the attention from her.

"You're overreacting," he'd said over and over. I'd accused him of having an "emotional affair" at a minimum, something he denied until the end. Maybe it wasn't.

I'd told Steve I hated him, and I didn't think we would ever be the same again. Steve would say volumes with his actions and hurtful one-liners, and I could say volumes in anger with words I could never take back.

I'd cried so hard in the bathroom that night that I had a coughing fit and vomited. Some may think that was a stupid thing to consider the last straw. It was just the tip of the iceberg though. I don't expect everyone to understand, and I relive this conversation from my viewpoint much differently than he probably does. I know I wasn't right in the way I dealt with a lot of what's about to come. But I'd known one thing for certain that night: those fateful texts were the blatant in-your-face messages confirming my marriage had been in trouble for a long time.

CHAPTER 16

THE DARK NIGHT

'D WOKEN UP THE NEXT morning and started pacing the house while Steve was still sleeping, wondering if I could even pull it together for work or if I should just stay home. I didn't want to see Steve. I didn't want to look him in the face. I was so hurt and angry. I did the only thing I knew how to do well. I went to work.

I went through the motions. I set my bag down at my desk, logged into my computer, sighed at the mountain of emails from DC already since they were three hours ahead of us on the West Coast, opened my desk drawer, grabbed my mug, and walked next door to the coffee machine. Adam, an agent in my squad, was making coffee. I wasn't standing by the machine five seconds before I blurted out, "Adam, I think Steve and I are done."

Poor Adam. I didn't make it a habit of airing my personal problems all over the office. He was a good sport. "Mel, if you need to go home, we can handle this here. Go do what you need to do."

"I don't know what to do. I think I'm in shock, and I couldn't just sit at home all day stewing about it."

"I understand. Well, if you need to talk or that changes, let us know, okay?"

I nodded, and he went to our office while I held back tears next to the coffee machine. With a fresh cup brewed, I told myself it was time to work, and I did my job.

My parents encouraged us to get some help and do what it took to try to rebuild and repair what had been lost and broken. Steve's mom, on the other hand, told Steve that I was the insecure one and that the texts in question weren't that bad. In other words, she wasn't encouraging Steve to work it out or to do what needed to be done to save his marriage. She cast blame without knowing anything. She told him, "Well, she can't be too shaken up about it because she went to work."

That, of course, infuriated me when Steve told me, and I lashed out at his mom, basically telling her, "You're not helping anything by assuming you know the whole story. Unless you're going to say something helpful or constructive about how Steve and I can work on our marriage, I suggest you butt out." Right or wrong, I was done with her attitude toward me.

We'd decided to get some counseling. Steve said he didn't want our marriage to be over. I didn't want my marriage to be over either. He'd also supposedly cut things off with Off-Road Cadet. In the meantime, I'd started at the Reagan Protective Division (RPD) with a heavy heart on August 9, 2015.

From the moment I officially started at RPD, I realized I had been given a gift at a very opportune time. I, along with four other Los Angeles Field Office agents, started on the same day, and we were welcomed with open arms. The vibe, morale, and attitudes of the agents lifted my spirits, at least in the workplace.

RPD agents were often called Reagan Rejects by the bigger protection details because they assumed the RPD agents were just a bunch of lazy beach bums who didn't like to do real protection work. I quickly learned that was not the case at all. Without exception, the agents on RPD chose to forego DC assignments and the likelihood of a future promotion for the betterment of their families. They were not lazy agents. They'd been handed the same gift I'd received: an aptly timed opportunity to avoid a life-altering move.

Being on RPD was easy. We rotated through the shifts each month, meaning one month of graveyards, one month of afternoon shift, and one month of morning shift. It was predictable and steady, something I hadn't experienced at all in the previous eight years.

Mrs. Reagan was in her nineties and didn't go out very often. Most people came to her, including her doctor, hairdresser, nail stylist, and others. Aside from screening packages and mail and monitoring the perimeter of her home in Bel Air, California, there wasn't a lot to do.

The house itself was old and dated, but the history within those walls was a sight to see. Even though it was a little creepy to walk through the halls to double-check all the locks and windows late at night, the art on the walls, photographs on the shelves, and the decorative items from all over the world were spectacular. *If only these rooms could talk,* I thought.

Mrs. Reagan called our command post phone semifrequently. Our command post was right next to her bedroom, and she usually had a question about her schedule that day. She also had her favorite longtime member of the detail named Troy who she asked about every time that phone rang.

"Is Troy there?"

"Not right now, ma'am. Is there something I can help you with?" I'd say, remembering how intimidating she was at Betty Ford's funeral when I'd hit the wrong button on the elevator much to her displeasure.

"I'm afraid not," she'd reply and hang up. She came across as curt most of the time, but she was never mean. She and I never had a personal conversation, and I'm pretty sure she never knew my name.

Being on a predictable schedule allowed Steve and I to make a couple of appointments to see a counselor. The counselor was nice, but none of the sessions went as I'd expected. I had never been to counseling before except once in college, and it was a joke. I'd thought she would ask us really tough questions and force us to talk about what we were feeling. I'd wanted to make progress or at least have those breakthroughs I'd heard about.

Instead, it seemed like Steve did what he always did: charmed everyone in the room but me. The therapist seemed a little irritated that we were there over some silly text messages, but when I'd tried to say it was way more than that, Steve admitted that he had made a mistake and wanted to fix the damage. "I feel terrible that I hurt her," he said. I said I missed Steve and I missed how we used to be. I mentioned the Tuesday date nights that weren't happening anymore. I told Steve I was always home on Tuesdays, and it clearly wasn't a priority to him. Steve promised to fix that, and by the time we got to that line of discussion, our hour was over.

"You need to make time for each other, and, Steve, you need to remember that if something is a big deal to one of you, it needs to be addressed as a big deal by both of you."

Nothing constructive or good came from any of the sessions we went to together. I felt numb all the time. I was just surviving again like in 2010 and 2011. I went through the motions of life, trying desperately to avoid an outburst and figure out how to prove to Steve that I was worth it. But try as I might, I was barely functioning. One day Steve and I would be hugging and crying, making promises that we would fix what had been damaged. The next day we might be okay. But it was inevitable that another fight was pending. When was it going to stop? When would I know if we were beyond repair?

"Mel, I'm not going to be the one to say it's over. I'm not giving up. If we are done, it's because you say we are," he'd said one day. *But your actions don't reflect that. You gave up a long time ago. Just because you verbally say something doesn't make it true.*

"I shouldn't have to beg you to act like you love me or beg you to want to spend time with me," I'd said as I began to cry again. I just wanted to crawl into bed and stay there until my heart didn't feel so heavy and my body didn't feel so foggy.

"I DO LOVE YOU!" Steve rarely raised his voice to me, but when he did, it was not in a loving way.

We had stopped going to the counselor together, and it wasn't long before something bad happened. I call it the Dark Night. I'm not proud of the Dark Night. But the Dark Night is a pivotal point in my life, a shameful moment I will regret forever. It was the night I recognized the monster that had grown in me, the monster of anger turned to utter disdain.

It was the night I hit my husband.

We had been fighting again, and I'd lost my temper... again. I said a lot of horrible things to him that night.

"I hate you!" I would slam doors and stomp around the house.

"I hope you die alone." My finger would be shaking in his face.

"I can't wait till karma bites you in the ass."

"I hate you for using me all these years!"

"I hate you for not having my back!"

"I hate you for making me feel undesirable!"

"I don't know what I ever saw in you. You were full of shit that day in Savannah."

"So much for not turning into your father. You followed right into his footsteps, didn't you?"

I would go on and on and on, wishing for an apology. But mostly, I wanted him to hurt like he'd hurt me.

Some people are proud of themselves when they tell someone off exactly the way they intended to. Kind of like those times in the shower when you envision how the conversation will go, and then it goes exactly that way in person. I was good at having an eloquent temper. But I found that after an ugly argument, I would wake up the next day full of guilt and shame. For a long time, I assured myself that he deserved every word and tongue lashing.

What we know trumps what we feel, and I knew my words were hateful and unnecessary to the situation. He was already hurting in his own way. How we react in anger says a lot about us. We think we are incapable of certain actions, but anger has a way of shocking us.

It's frightening to realize I was capable of hurting the person I loved more than anyone in the world. It was frightening that I could disdain him with the same intensity. In that moment, the moment my arm swung and knocked him near his left ear, I hated myself. I hated the monster I'd become.

I never thought in a million years I would hit Steve. Never. I had been angry with him, but I never wanted to physically harm him in any way. I don't even remember making the decision to hit him. It just happened. I know that sounds like a cop-out, but it's the truth. I'd swung before I realized what I was doing. I was out of control, and in the moment of impact, I knew it.

He just stared at me, his hand coming to his ear. I can't even imagine the thoughts that must have been going through his head. I immediately apologized. I apologized continuously for a long time. I felt like a worthless monster. *You deserve everything that's happening to you.* I knew no matter how badly he'd treated me or how many times he'd hurt me, I was wrong to do what I did. It didn't matter that the physical damage was minimal. He was a tough guy. I'd crossed a line that should never have been crossed.

My biggest regrets in life to date are the things I said and did to Steve in anger. The shame followed me like a ton of bricks strapped to my back. I begged him for forgiveness and apologized over and over again. He did use the Dark Night as leverage, his way of pointing out that my actions were worse than anything he'd ever done to me.

After that moment, I ceased to be a catch. I became the wife who hit her husband in anger. I was not only afraid of what others would think of me by revealing that dark moment, but I was afraid that action would taint my worth forever. How could anyone care what I had to say if I was capable of hitting my spouse?

I think about that night sometimes. I think about his face. He just sat there. He'd been sitting there the whole time, refusing to speak. Just quiet. He wasn't going to participate in my tantrum. Don't reward bad behavior, they say. His face haunts me because it was like looking in a mirror. The look he gave me perfectly reflected how I felt about myself. He hated me as much as I hated myself.

I went to bed that night wishing I would die in my sleep and never have to wake up and face myself (or Steve) ever again. It was the first time I actually thought of suicide as a legitimate option. It would make the pain stop, I thought. The Dark Night confirmed I was out of control. I didn't want to be this person. I detested abusers, rolling my eyes at their stupid apologies.

"Oh, baby, I'll never hit you again. I promise."

I was even using their lines. I disgusted myself.

"Oh my God, Steve! I am so sorry! I'm so sorry! Are you okay? I promise I will never ever do that again." How pathetic it sounded: I'll never do it again. That's what they all said, and then the victim winds up in the hospital, the abuser saying he or she deserved the brutal beating.

When I'd woken up, I knew I needed help. That angry, violent person could not be the real me. I made a vow to myself to never ever underestimate myself or my capabilities, especially in anger. I had the ability to control my behavior, and it was about time I started.

CHAPTER 17

WHAT'S YOUR SITREP?

SITREP: Short for Situation Report

THE SECRET SERVICE AND OTHER government agencies use a lot of canned language to quickly relay information over the radios. Sometimes it felt like we weren't speaking English because of the piles of acronyms at our disposal. Brevity is crucial though, and no one likes a chatterbox. Keep it short. Keep it clean.

Motorcades involve a lot of radio communication. Between the lane changes, turns, and updates, there's enough talking. Periodically the lead agent provides SITREPs to the motorcade. Basically, the SITREP is a status update as it relates to the arrival at the next site or event. By the time the motorcade is about to arrive, the SITREP must be "all clear for arrival" or the protectee isn't coming. The site agent cannot say "all clear" if a random delivery truck is making an eighteen-point turn because he was told by officers and agents at the checkpoint to come back after the event. If a demonstration has decided to take over the intersection and block the motorcade, the site agent should not give an "all clear" SITREP.

If it's not all clear, don't say it is. It's common sense with a protection mindset but often terribly executed when the same concept is applied to my personal life.

After the Dark Night, I asked a couple of people at the office if the Secret Service had a counseling program like a lot of police departments. I was told to contact a lady named Audrey in the Los Angeles Field Office. She was one of the office managers and a kind soul. On August 24, 2015, I sent her the following message on Facebook:

> "Happy Birthday, Audrey! I hope you had a wonderful day!
>
> I had a quick question for you. I talked to Britney the other day, and she said she thought you might have the answer to my question. Does the USSS have any sort of program that offers counseling or have a contract with a company locally that does? My husband's police department does. He has ten sessions per year covered by the department at this one location. I am asking because I would like to talk to someone and thought maybe my work had something like that. Please keep it between us (Brit knows), but my husband and I are having problems. I feel like we aren't getting anywhere at the one place… been there three times. Thinking I would like to talk to someone on my own. Maybe it would help me work through some things that have happened. So figured I would see if work covered anything like that before I start googling places around me. Thanks, Audrey!"

That Facebook message was the start of one of the best decisions I have ever made: the decision to admit I was not okay. I had finally given myself an honest SITREP, and I was not "all clear."

I knew I was depressed when I sent the message. I figured the depression was a by-product of my marital problems, but deep down I thought maybe the depression had been around before that. I was afraid asking for help would affect my job. I really didn't want my employers to know what was going on, and at that point, only a couple of very close friends knew a summary of my recent life events. I never told a soul about hitting Steve though.

Help came quickly after I sent the message. Audrey provided contact information for the Secret Service Employee Assistance Program (EAP). I had probably been briefed about this program's existence at some point, but like so many others, I didn't think it would ever apply to me. Obviously, that was an egotistical assumption.

I contacted the lead doctor at the EAP. The Secret Service might have had a slew of issues surrounding employee morale and dysfunction among the agency's top leaders, but they did one thing right, and that was to hire the people at the EAP. From the moment I spoke with them, I knew I had made the right decision. I told them my marriage was falling apart, and I was headed down with it. I said I needed to get some help.

"So, Melanie, what kind of counselor are you looking for?"

"Well, I guess I would like to talk to someone who's actually married, maybe someone a little older. I don't want to talk to someone fresh out of school. I hope that doesn't sound judgmental."

"No, Melanie. That's why I'm here: to find someone you're comfortable speaking with."

Within just a couple of days, the EAP contacted me with a list of three possible counselors in my area who fit the criteria and took my insurance. In addition, they'd made contact with one counselor who made herself available the very next day (or possibly the day after that). I couldn't believe it.

I cried during the entire first counseling session. Audrey would later tell me, "Been there… cleansing the soul is all." My hurt and sadness had been manifesting itself as anger for so long. It was refreshing to be real for once, to let the sadness be what it was: crushing.

I left the initial session feeling drained, a little embarrassed, and relieved. I don't know how counselors do it. I was in the same room listening to myself talk, and I was drained. I imagine she needed a nap and a cup of coffee when she was done listening to my bubbling explosion of feelings.

I went back to her, and I kept getting help. After a couple of sessions, my therapist said something I was dreading: "I think you should be evaluated by a psychiatrist for depression." Gut punch.

My response was not positive.

"A psychiatrist? Are *you* crazy? I'm depressed because my marriage is falling apart. I can handle it. Look at me. I'm crying and talking and getting it all out with you here. I don't need a medical doctor to prescribe me a 'happy pill' because that's not going to make the circumstances go away. Screw that. I'm not taking a pill. Plus I have to report psychiatric medications to my workplace, and I'm sure that will go over about as well as a high-maintenance foreign dignitary extending his stay in Los Angeles over Christmas. What if I got into a shooting or a fight at work? I can just see the headlines now: 'Secret Service Agent Involved in Recent Shooting Was Clinically Depressed.' Not me. I'm not that agent."

My therapist was visibly irritated with my assumptions and uneducated naivety. But she sighed a patient sigh and reasoned with me.

"You may not need medication, but if the doctor suggests it, I think you should follow the doctor's advice."

I was angry at that point, but she went on convincingly.

"A medicated, depressed agent with an imploding personal life—but one who's learning and practicing effective coping mechanisms while dealing with her problems—is an effective and efficient agent, coworker, and protector. A depressed agent with an imploding personal life with ineffective, unhealthy, and destructive coping mechanisms is not going to be as effective and efficient in a crisis situation."

I hoped she was right, and I hoped the Secret Service would agree with her if it came to that.

I didn't contact a psychiatrist right away. I started seeing this therapist in late August or early September 2015. When I finally got around to it in late October, I walked into the initial appointment skeptically. I looked around the waiting room at the patients. One was scribbling away furiously in a journal, oblivious to anyone else's presence. Another was swaying back and forth in his chair, avoiding any and all eye contact. Another looked like he was ready to jump out of his skin. In front of me was a teenage girl sitting quietly.

I told myself I didn't belong with these crazy people. After all, I had been to several mental hospitals to interview patients about threats made against protectees. I was the one who spoke with the doctors, had memorized the most common medications, and then wrote investigative reports about it. I was the investigator, not a fellow patient. My judgment is yet another cringe-worthy reminder of my state of mind at the time.

The doctor was professional but not overly friendly. She stuck to the point and even said early on, "So you're here to get meds, right?"

I quickly filled her in. "No, I do not want to take meds. I'm only here to appease my therapist, and I am just desperate enough to sit in this chair right now."

I'd researched antidepressant medications extensively prior the appointment, and one terrible side effect resonated in my brain: weight gain. My eating disorder history was at the forefront of my mind. I'd relapsed and had been purging occasionally and continued to excessively exercise. If I gained weight taking happy pills, I most definitely would not be happy. Online forums among patients contained horror stories of excessive weight gain despite healthy eating and other disturbing side effects. Obviously, an online forum is probably not the best source for research, but their testimonials had me terrified of what would happen to me if I were prescribed an antidepressant.

After forty-five minutes with the psychiatrist, I'd been asked a million questions, canned questions that needed to be asked but sounded so formal and rehearsed.

"Do you experience feelings of hopelessness?"

"Sometimes."

"Do you ever think about suicide?"

"Not really." I didn't tell her I had thought about it several times as an option if I couldn't get a handle on this crushing heartache.

"Do you feel like harming others when you feel hopeless?"

"No."

It went on and on.

I walked out of the office with a prescription for an antidepressant. I homed in on one particular medication prior to the appointment, one less likely to cause weight gain. After all, I was a planner. I tried never to enter a situation unprepared.

I filled the prescription and let it sit on the counter for a few days. I dreaded calling the Employee Assistance Program (EAP) to report my prescription. Would I lose my security clearance? Would I be placed on light duty? Would people think I was unfit to be a Secret Service agent? Assuming the worst possible outcome, I picked up the phone. The doctor at the EAP said something that has stuck with me to this day.

"Melanie, you would be surprised how many special agents and Uniformed Division officers struggle with depression. Many suffer from anxiety in addition to that. It's staggering, and you are not alone. This job is not easy on anyone, and you shouldn't feel ashamed for any of this. You're doing the right thing to get help. That's something many agents and officers never do."

My mind was put at ease, and I started taking the meds. My doctor was requested to write a letter to the Secret Service staff doctor to determine if I was fit for duty.

When I gave the doctor the information at my next appointment, she was kind. I'd actually grown to appreciate her directness and personality.

"I'll write the letter," she said and placed the paperwork on her desk. Whatever she wrote satisfied the clearing physician.

"Is my depression situational because of what's going on in my life right now, or do you think this is something I'm going to be dealing with for the rest of my life?" While undiagnosed, I suspected depression might run in my family.

"It's too soon to tell. But keep doing what you're doing. You do want to get better, right?"

"Yes."

I'd be lying if I said the meds didn't help a little. My therapist had said they might "take the edge off" just enough to help me cope and make the best decisions. I was still embarrassed for taking them. I was embarrassed that I couldn't handle a divorce on my own; I felt weak. I still thought I was less of an agent because of the meds. What would people think?

Steve and I were still functioning within our usual yo-yo, the ups and downs so chaotic I couldn't keep track of where we were. I knew we weren't getting better, but I think we both knew that whatever was happening was serious.

Steve had said I was "so much better" on the medication. "I'm glad you're taking them," he said. *Well, aren't you just the picture of a supportive and loving husband,* I thought sarcastically. Instead, I had stayed quiet, and that was probably a good thing.

I continued going to counseling sessions, but antidepressants aren't a magic happy pill. I didn't eat very much, and I was still purging on occasion for the first time since 2008. I felt like a drunk going off the bandwagon after years of sobriety.

I started avoiding being at home, which is something I'm not proud of. I think I already knew deep down I was fighting a losing battle to save this marriage. I accused Steve of giving up, but I can see now that my actions were also giving off a defeated vibe. We continued to have opposite schedules now that I was working protection full time, so it was easy to avoid him, but I hated being in that empty house when he wasn't there. As confusing and tormented as I was, I missed him when I was home alone.

I spent an unhealthy amount of time at Krav Maga classes in Downtown LA. I trained there almost every day, sometimes twice a day. I'd go before work, and I'd go back after work. One instructor even commented that he thought I was training too much. I knew he was right, but being there took my mind off my personal and professional life. It was my escape, the only place where there was no Steve and no reminders of my dysfunction.

Sometimes instructors and other members would try to talk to me, and I avoided anything more than small talk. Many of them knew about my job by then, and I didn't want to talk about it, and that's typically all they asked about. To me, it was literally the only thing interesting about me, and when I was there, I wanted to forget who Melanie Lentz was. I wanted to have tunnel vision for just a little while and have fun punching a heavy bag and practicing some techniques in the mat room. Heaven forbid, someone would actually try to talk to me about my messed-up life.

Maybe turning to martial arts was better than turning to drugs and alcohol. But it wasn't a healthy coping mechanism regardless. It was just a way to delay facing reality.

I had the good sense to tell my counselor that I was struggling again, and she referred me to an eating disorder specialist. I know it helped to talk things out with someone who specialized in people like me. The new specialist had suffered from anorexia in her past, so she had more than book knowledge about what I was dealing with.

For the first time in my life, I was honest with someone about what I was doing behind closed doors. That honesty became freeing to me. I'd been intentionally deceptive about my disordered eating. Vulnerability was tough, but I was tired of hiding.

By seeing an eating disorder specialist, I was able to tell Steve I was getting the help he'd been asking me to get for years. It was something I threw back in his face.

"I'm doing everything you've asked me to do, Steve! Clearly you think I'm the problem, so rest assured. I'm a medicated and quiet shell of a human for you now. Are you happy?"

"Oh, yeah? You've done everything? You never went to the Catholic classes like you said you would."

"What else, Steve? Let's hear it." I threw my defeated hands into the air. "What more do you want? I don't have anything else to give! I've told you a million times I'm not the Energizer Bunny. You were lying when you said you loved me despite my flaws. You didn't tell me that every flaw would be held against me until the end of time. You expect perfection, Steve, because you're a narcissist. That seventeen-year-old girl you saw on the first day of college was not your perfect little imaginary soul mate after all. Maybe that's why you have to get your ego-fueled attention fix from someone practically that age." Needless to say, I continued to hurt with my words while he hurt me with silence.

I didn't want to hate Steve or anyone. I wanted to love and be loved, but I was nowhere near ready for that because I hated myself. I didn't know how to love myself because all I saw was the lunatic wife taking a swing at her husband.

I told my supervisor at the Reagan detail the shortest possible version about what was going on with me. I figured he should be informed in case the Security Clearance Division contacted him about me. I didn't want him to be blindsided. My shift also knew what was going on but not in great detail. They were all exceptionally supportive. All those agents were married, and they assured me that marital problems were not a foreign concept to any of them. They felt sorry for me, but then again, they only knew the put-together side of me that knew how to turn off my personal problems when I was working.

"Your husband is an idiot if he lets you go. You don't need to be with a fool, Mel."

By Thanksgiving 2015, Steve and I were hardly talking. I had started journaling, and those entries are haunting to me because I remember the feelings but not necessarily the conversations I wrote about. I wrote about Steve saying I didn't respect him. I wrote about him telling me his greatest fear was not being good enough. And then the next entry would be about him initiating sex followed by an entry about not talking to each other for a couple of days. No wonder I was in a haze. The yo-yo of emotions was nauseating.

The Reagan detail supervisors always tried to ensure agents had at least one major holiday off to spend with their families. Since I had only been on the detail since August, most of the agents had long since put in their leave requests for Christmas. Most of the agents had kids, and they wanted to spend Christmas with them. That was fine with me.

Since my immediate family was out of state, my parents and my sister asked to meet in Las Vegas for Thanksgiving. Steve and I had to drive separately due to work schedules. We had tickets to Cirque de Soleil the first night, and Steve said he would leave in plenty of time to make it to the show.

I had this sinking feeling that he might not show up. I even thought to myself, "If he's going to leave me, this is when he'll do it." But he came.

My sister and I got dressed up for the show. She did my hair, and I felt pretty that night. Before we left for the show, I looked in the mirror. *Oh no,* I thought. *I'm wearing tinted lip gloss. Steve hates lipstick and lip gloss. I need to get rid of this before he gets here.* I rubbed it all off. He would never kiss me with lipstick or gloss on. "Ew, get that crap off your lips," he'd say.

We all had fun at the shows, but I sensed some awkwardness among the group, as if we were just ignoring the elephant in the room and going through the motions. My parents were incredibly worried about me. I knew that. When it was time to leave, I realized how lonely I'd become in all this.

The week after this trip, on December 2, 2015, Steve and I were both home as I got ready for work. I looked into his eyes, and I just knew: he was done. I walked to the side door to leave and looked at him. "I know you're done, and I'm going to make you say it."

He looked at me with his usual blank stare, the stare that said "screw you" louder than any words could ever say. It was the look of disgust I'd grown accustomed to, yet no one but me had seen. He didn't say a word as I walked out the door.

That night we decided to end our marriage.

"I'm not in love with who you've become," I said.

"I'm not in love with who *you've* become," he said.

We were both in agreement. We were beyond repair. He moved in with his mom shortly after, and the papers were filed just a couple of weeks later. Dissolving the marriage was easier than starting it.

A day or two before this marriage-ending conversation, Steve found out he'd passed his probationary period at the police department and would obtain career status in a few days. Maybe the timing was coincidental, but I felt incredibly used. That's what hurt the most. I'd stuck by him at his worst. When I progressed to my worst, he was gone. The easier option was to let me go rather than love me as I had loved him all those years he sat around, depressed in his own way.

But regardless of timing, the marriage was over. I thought my sadness would pass with the removal of my major stressors or triggers (as therapists call them). I was getting a divorce (marital stressor removed), and I was finally working protection full time at the Reagan detail (workplace stressor removed). I was wrong.

CHAPTER 18

SINGLE IN THE WILD

AFTER STEVE HAD MOVED OUT, I felt like a fish out of water. My empty ring finger felt naked, but the ring box in my sock drawer seemed to scream at me every time I opened the drawer. He'd left the dogs with me, saying, "They need to be with their mama." His things were gone for the most part. He'd spent the next few months taking random small loads from the garage. Even with his stuff removed, it still seemed like he should have been there. The first week he was gone, I woke up feeling like he was sleeping next to me. But when I rolled over to hug him before getting up, reality stung: I was alone and single for the first time in almost ten years.

When Steve and I would hear about a single friend or coworker's relationship issues, we'd usually say, "I'm so glad I'm not single. It's a jungle out there. I would hate to be dating today." Now I'd been thrust into the jungle, and I wasn't sure I was cut out for life in the wild.

Friends and coworkers were full of well-meaning advice and reassurances.

"Oh, Mel, you're going to be single for a minimum of five seconds. Someone is going to snatch you up."

"Your husband is a complete fool to let you go. If I were single, I'd have asked you out yesterday."

"You need to get laid as soon as possible so you can move on."

"You should give yourself time to heal before you think about dating again."

"Be careful with the first person you fall for after the divorce. It probably won't work out, and when it doesn't, it's going to bring back all the feelings of rejection you had during the divorce."

I was surprised at how quickly my coworkers started coming out of the woodwork too. Guys from the Los Angeles office, many of whom had moved on to protection details, started calling and expressing interest. Most of them I knew to be playboys, especially when they traveled. It was their promiscuity and talk about their conquests that made me thankful I wasn't single. *Good Lord, it's savage out there.*

Without exception, they all basically said the same thing.

"Mel, you're an awesome girl, and I like you a lot. I know I've been a jerk to women in the past. But I'm at the point in my life where I want to settle down with a nice girl and have a family. I don't know if you'd be interested in me or find me attractive, but I'm interested in you and find you attractive."

I was flattered by their interest and grateful that they had enough respect (hopefully) to avoid making me just another notch in their headboard. I turned every single one of them down with the same basic rejection: "Steve just moved out. The ink isn't dry on the divorce papers. I haven't processed all this yet. I need some time to heal."

But what I was really feeling was this:

I don't want to be the nice girl you settle down with and start a family. I want us to be enough together. I have never felt like I was good enough… or just simply enough. I don't want anyone who treats me like the boring safe bet you seek out because you think it's what you should do after being a womanizer for so many years.

I continued to go to counseling and see the psychiatrist. The psychiatrist said she wanted me to stay on the medication for at least nine months before trying to wean off them. I couldn't wait to have that discussion. After the holidays, I was reminded that I was still a patient during one office visit.

"Hello, Melanie," the psychiatrist said. "Have a seat. Please close the door."

"How are you, Doctor?" I said.

"I'm well. I just got back from vacation with my family."

"Oh, how nice! Where did you go?"

She looked at me like I had two heads. There was no way she was going to tell me where she took her family on vacation. She was probably afraid telling a patient her vacation whereabouts would wind up being the sequel to the movie *What About Bob?* with Bill Murray and Richard Dreyfuss. Bill Murray's character was Richard Dreyfuss's psychiatric patient, and Murray hilariously socially engineered his way into his shrink's family vacation.

Ah, yes, I was a patient now, and that was truly humbling.

Life at Mrs. Reagan's detail remained steady and sane. As angry as I was about the timing of the divorce and my transfer, I think God was looking out for me. When everything blew up after the Off-Road Cadet debacle, I didn't stop taking the birth control after Steve's birthday as planned. While I believe every baby and life is precious, it was for the best that I was not pregnant already. If the divorce had happened sooner, I might have backed out of the local transfer altogether and waited for a DC assignment to escape.

But as it happened, my transfer orders had come out already, and I was still finishing my birth control pack. At Mrs. Reagan's, I was surrounded by a bunch of great guys and one other awesome female agent who loved their families and knew that there was more to life than the job. Most of them knew the importance of work-life balance, and I believe they offered a healthy perspective and insight during this time. The vibe in the Los Angeles Field Office was very career oriented, and the advice I would have received would likely have been aimed at convincing me to take a DC transfer.

I don't know how I feel about concepts like predestination, luck, and fate, but I know being on Mrs. Reagan's detail was a gift I will always appreciate.

Since Steve was a police officer in the town I lived in, I couldn't escape him. After all the years sharing bank accounts and space, it seemed like there was constantly something to communicate about: insurance, wills, life insurance, a random trinket of his I'd found, seeing the dogs, mail, et cetera. I'd see him at streetlights while he was on patrol. Once I saw him responding to a call at the grocery store. I'd see his car parked at the police department when I went to the library next door. Sometimes if I was home at night, I'd see a patrol car drive past the house in the middle of the night and wonder if he was assigned to my area that night.

We were amicable for the most part, but we still bickered when he would stop by to get mail. One day he said, "My friends are telling me I'm so much better and happier now that we're not together." We needed a clean break. We just couldn't see each other without saying something hurtful. Seeing him made it worse.

I started paying attention to articles, television, and social media information about dating. Steve and I didn't really date. We hung out at school, went running, and went surfing with friends. I don't remember Steve ever picking me up with flowers hidden behind his back and taking me to dinner. And before that, I never had a healthy romantic relationship. The last time

I'd gone on an actual date was when I was getting my bachelor's degree ten or more years prior.

It seemed like so much had changed, and there was a lot of conflicting information. If a guy asked me out, did I offer to pay for my own dinner? One person would say, "Absolutely not. Chivalry isn't dead. He can pay for your dinner." Then the next person would say, "You don't need a man, and you make your own money. Pay for your own dinner and treat each other as equals." *Which is it, for goodness' sake?*

Everyone was online dating. I cringe when I admit that I made fun of people in college who were online dating. It seemed like the sort of thing loners and nerds would do. I suppose I'd heard friends and coworkers talking about online dating over the years; I just didn't think it would ever apply to me. Plus online dating had taken on a new, superficial form. Now a profile was reduced to a heavily edited photo and a two-sentence emoji-filled bio. Swipe left for "no" and right for "yes." Easy.

Huh? Why can't I just meet some nice dude at the farmers' market? We'll reach for the same avocado and have a face-to-face conversation about how much we love dogs and guacamole. Is that too much to ask?

I thought I was going to have to conform eventually though. But I couldn't think of one single person who would say "I'm seeking a divorced, thirtysomething female with three dogs and an eating disorder history. Oh, and if she could be in therapy for depression as well as the eating disorder, that would be great." I know we all have our own faults and baggage to bring to the table. But I thought mine might be too much.

In January 2016, shortly after Steve had moved out, a friend said, "I've been on three Bumble or Tinder dates in the past week. You've got to get out there and figure out what you like and what you want. This is how it's done now."

There was a part of me that wanted to get back out there and prove to myself that I was desirable. I wasn't going to be an ugly spinster with a million pets.

Being in Los Angeles meant my dating jungle was exceptionally wild. Swiping right got me a smorgasbord of different characters. One guy invited me to a spicy pool party that would turn into a big group sex fest. *Wow. Wait. What?* Another guy said he was looking for a threesome for him and his wife. *I'm not really into crowded beds, and I'm not good at sharing, if you know what I mean.* Another guy merely sent me his length and girth measurements so I knew his penis was a giant before we even had a conversation. He had a beard in his photo, so I sent a smartass comment like, "Dude, since you have your tape measure out, how long is that beard?" What in the world? *I don't think I'm cut out for this dating life,* I'd think as I clicked out of the app and blocked a few people.

However, since I'd never been a single Secret Service agent, I did not realize I would have a large group of big brothers when I did meet someone. Most of the Reagan detail guys had been married for many years, and they were fascinated with this new swipe-right dating life. But they were very protective of me, and I was appreciative.

"Seriously, Mel. Let me see his picture. Okay, good. Now where are you going? What time? Do you need one of us to do a drive-by to make sure you're okay? Maybe we should have a code word you could text us if you need to get out of there in a hurry. Better yet. Give one of us his cell phone number. If you turn up missing, we'll track the phone."

I did see someone for a short time. The first evening I met him, I had to work a midnight shift at Mrs. Reagan's house afterward. When I walked into the command post, the guys teased me a little. "Aw, look at her face. She's all glowy." It was fun, and as much as I tried to keep my emotions casual, I fell for him. I took it hard when it didn't work out. I guess the advice to be careful with the first person after Steve was sound advice I hadn't heeded.

Everything romantic around me seemed so superficial, a sad, shallow reality that only further confirmed my status as a human being: lost and confused. The swipe-right culture proved to be more juvenile games and guesswork than any of my previous juvenile quasi relationships.

I wish someone would have warned me that things might get worse before they'd get better, but I doubt I would have listened to that person. *Fasten your seat belt, Mel. It's not getting better just yet.*

CHAPTER 19

THE ART OF SILENCE

"I love you so very much I don't even mind that life made me wait so long to find you. The waiting only made the finding sweeter."

— Ronald Reagan

O N March 6, 2016, I woke to a ringing cell phone. My heart sank. Somehow I knew what the caller would say before I answered.

"The Mrs. passed away a few minutes ago," my colleague said. We referred to Nancy Reagan as Mrs. R. or "the Mrs."

I had been instructed to meet at the prearranged funeral home in nearby Santa Monica. When I arrived, other agents were posted around the building along with local police officers. Satellite trucks and press were milling about outside, the whole scene an image of rehearsed chaos.

My supervisor gathered my shift into a small room. Another shift was on their way with Mrs. Reagan's body, and we would relieve them when they arrived so they could go home.

"Guys, we've known this day would come, and we will protect her like always until she's laid to rest," he said.

We nodded.

"Someone needs to be in the room while they prepare her body."

All eyes widened at his statement.

"I'll do it," I said after a brief pause. I was the only female agent on this shift. In fact, there were only two female agents on the entire detail. Mrs. Reagan wasn't a grandmotherly figure to me. In fact, I didn't know her well, and we never had an actual conversation outside of logistical snippets, usually from the other end of a telephone line. Regardless, I'd like to think she would have appreciated my presence, my subtle way of respecting her womanly dignity. I wound up staying in the room for most of the preparations.

I made my way to the embalming room. I knew where it was from touring it when I was assigned to Mrs. Reagan's demise security plan. It looked the way I remembered except a beautiful mahogany casket was sitting ominously in the corner.

The garage door attached to the embalming room creaked open, and the hearse pulled into the garage. A small wooden casket was brought into the room. There were two morticians assigned to Mrs. Reagan's body preparations. The longtime Reagan staff members ushered everyone else out of the room, and I moved out of the way to let the men do their work.

As the men started preparing their equipment and tools, I stared at the casket. I thought about Christmastime. She had attended a neighbor's holiday party, and I drove her to the event. We all piled into the minivan with a wheelchair ramp, and her nurse dressed up as her date. Troy, her favorite member of her detail, secured her wheelchair into the van as my boss took the seat next to me in the front.

"You're looking lovely tonight, ma'am," Troy said.

"Oh, really? I just threw this old outfit together." Her eyes twinkled as they continued their witty bantering. She was smiling and seemed happy. Her son, Ron, came along as well.

When we arrived at the party, her nurse climbed out of the van and wheeled her backward down the ramp. She was facing toward me as she was backed out. She looked at me, smirked, and then said, "Well… bye!" followed by a quick wink. I just stared wide-eyed like an idiot as she went into the party, but maybe I said something polite. She wasn't normally so feisty around me.

Being assigned to her detail did not change or soften my fear of her. I remembered her icy stare in the elevator at Betty Ford's funeral when I had pushed the wrong button on the elevator. She was very direct and assertive, and as one of her longtime staffers would so aptly put it our first day at the funeral home, everyone learned the art of silence when dealing with her. I might have thought I knew what she needed, but I was always wrong, and she had no problem telling me so from the other end of the command post telephone line. It was a self-correcting error on my part after my first conversation with her. Listen first, silly.

The morticians moved beside the casket like bodyguards.

I'm not prepared for this, I thought. But then, how did one prepare?

The next moment is sealed in my brain forever: the moment the casket was opened. The inner gasp and the emotional response: "This is not normal. I can't Google how to mentally zone for this. What is my head supposed to do with what's about to happen?"

And then former First Lady Nancy Reagan's small body was gently lifted onto the table.

The embalming room was quiet for the most part. The two older gentlemen tasked with her body preparations were not new faces to the Secret Service. The same men had embalmed Ronald Reagan and other deceased Secret Service protectees.

I stood stone-faced, remaining vigilant. I was not concerned about the two men in the room, but there was some concern about photographs being snuck or people attempting to see this extremely private and sensitive process. It was a scene classified on a "need to be there" basis. Periodically one or both the two men would look at me and ask if I was okay. I always responded with a "yes," but my mind was going a mile a minute.

I tried several approaches. First I thought about the sanctity of life. Life can be taken away so quickly. I felt sorry for Mrs. R. She did not pass with family by her side, holding her hand with loving words as she took her last breaths. She died in her house with longtime house staff, a couple of her full-time nurses, and a handful of Secret Service agents in the command post.

While I will not claim to know the inner workings of her personal relationships with her children, I found it sad that none of them were there. It was admittedly a judgmental moment. I thought about when my grandmother had passed away a few years before. Death does not always come quickly, the death rattle breathing seeming to go on forever as my grandma's body had slowly shut down. All her four children, my grandpa, and some of the grandchildren were there.

Those thoughts were immediately replaced with the realization that I had not been there when my grandma took her last breath. I didn't want to see it. I didn't want to see her dead, for that to be my last memory of her. I wanted to remember her alive, and I chose to leave before that time came. I feared death, and the thought of dying with only paid staff present still made me sad. Obviously, there was a lot I did not know.

I thought about science. Prior to that date, I was relatively unfamiliar with the embalming process except that it was a preservation of sorts, an attempt to make the deceased look less deceased so the family could say goodbye. Despite the overall disconnect I felt from Mrs. Reagan, the process was still difficult to watch. Since I had a basic knowledge of human physiology, I chose to listen more carefully to what the men were saying.

They were the epitome of respectful and professional, communicating to each other in scientific terms. I understood most of their physiological references. I might have even asked a question or two about what they were doing. I got by for a while by thinking unemotionally, anatomically.

The whole process didn't take long the first day. When the initial portion was over, she was brought into a room where we would post up for the night. The midnight shift relieved the day shift, and I drove home, exhausted and drained. I would only be able to sleep a couple of hours because I had to be back in Santa Monica the next morning.

I arrived tired but heavily caffeinated the next day, and the preparations continued. She looked lovely and classy when everything was finished. She was dressed in a beautiful designer suit, and her wedding ring was the final touch before she was transferred into the big and shiny mahogany casket, identical to the one her husband was buried in years before.

At some point during that week, my boss informed some of us that we would be pallbearers for the private family funeral. I don't know if that was Mrs. R.'s wishes all along or if it was something the staff had decided on her behalf. It wasn't documented in any of the predetermined plans when I was in Protection Operations. *Why me?* I'd only been on her detail for eight months.

I don't know why I was selected. Maybe it was just because I was day shift and it worked out best that way. That's how a lot of assignments are doled out in the Secret Service: convenience. But either way, I knew what an honor it was to carry her casket.

On the day of the family funeral, I showed up at the funeral home in my best suit. The eight pallbearers were given a quick down-and-dirty tutorial about how to hold and carry the casket. I was a little nervous. I was the smallest one in the line and the only female. The casket was heavy despite Mrs. R.'s slight frame.

I cringe when I see the footage of us carrying that casket because most of the guys looked like big clumsy dudes stepping on each other's heels while we walked. It was awkward, and we didn't want to mess anything up.

The still photos that circulated in the media were a little better, but I looked angry in them compared to the others. But as I look at them now, I know that face was one of a woman who was trying desperately to hold it together. My unemotional switch was on, my personal life on hold, my emotions in the back seat, and I was just trying to do my job.

As soon as Mrs. R. was in the hearse after the family funeral, the day shift climbed in the motorcade. I was driving the vehicle behind the hearse, and my shift leader sat in the passenger seat, manning the radio. More agents filled the back seat as we always did when we protected someone. There was a protocol, and we were still following it even though we were in a motorcade with a hearse.

We drove to the Reagan Presidential Library that day. Aside from driving in a presidential motorcade a couple of times, this motorcade was an amazing one to be part of. The streets were lined with people, and overpasses were filled with signs. Local firemen and police officers were there with their vehicles' emergency lights flashing as a sign of respect.

During the drive, I made a comment about the crowd.

"Look at everyone. They're all staring at their phones as they take videos of the motorcade passing by. They're missing out on seeing life in real time. Instead, they'll review it later when they post it on social media. What a total disconnect. That's sad."

"Oh my God, you're right. Everyone is on their phones," my shift leader noted with his thumb hovering over the radio's button in case he needed to call anything out.

We'd comment on it the rest of the way to the library. Memories can be preserved with photos, but it's too easy to overlook what matters in real time when we're preoccupied with the preservation. Some memories need more appreciation than preservation.

When we arrived at the library, the funeral arrangements were in full swing with Secret Service and Reagan staff bustling about as they coordinated and prepped. Other protectees would be attending the larger funeral as well as many politicians and a few Hollywood types. In addition to that, there was a public viewing, which was not even a viewing at all because the only people who saw the open casket were family and close staff at the private funeral. I was amazed at the droves and droves of people who waited in line to walk around the casket covered in a beautiful white rose display. They called it paying their respects.

The agents and staff had taken a moment to pay their respects too. I never really understood what that meant, exactly. I followed the lead of those in front of me, taking a moment to bow my head next to the casket and continue down the line. It was uncomfortable for me because the second I found myself standing in front of the casket, I thought about her lying on that embalming room table at the funeral home and the loneliness of the whole scene. I didn't linger long. My discomfort must have been apparent because Joanne Drake, the Reagan Foundation's chief administrative officer, asked if I was okay afterward.

I'd been turning my heart off for several days by then, and I was starting to crack. I'd received news from my boss that I'd be receiving transfer orders to Washington DC to finish the full-time protection phase of my career, and the uncertainty of my future could not be addressed until this funeral was over. Panic mode was knocking on my door. Not only that, but I was driving from the San Gabriel Valley to Simi Valley every day for nine a.m. to nine p.m. shifts at the Reagan Library, leaving my house a little after five a.m. every day to avoid the awful Los Angeles commuter traffic so I could relieve the midnight shift on time. Then at nine p.m., I had a long drive back home. I was functioning on individually packaged after-dinner mints in my suit pocket and copious amounts of coffee and snacks at the little shop in the library.

Secret Service agents are well versed in the art of standing in one place for a long time. Some agents deliberately dehydrate themselves so they don't have to pee as often since breaks are a luxury. I always hated it when my stomach started growling at work. We were not allowed to eat while on post, but I always kept after-dinner mints in the inner pocket of my suit. Not the hard candy ones but the softer buttermint ones that don't melt slowly but can be chewed and swallowed in a hurry. As we rotated through posts, I would hand my colleagues a mint or two.

On the day of the official memorial service a couple of days later, the day-shift agents met at a Starbucks parking lot near the library. We'd been instructed to carpool because parking congestion was expected during the funeral. I was one of the first to arrive because I was coming from a longer distance and needed to beat traffic. I went inside to grab a coffee, undoubtedly not my first of the day. When I came out, other agents were starting to arrive, including the Ventura Resident Office's supervisor. He came up to our group with a man trailing behind him.

"Morning, guys," he said. "This is Tim McCarthy."

As the guys started shaking his hand and greeting him, I stole a glance at the supervisor. He must have read my "Why should I know this guy?" expression because he kindly said, "Mel, this is the agent who was shot with Reagan."

I immediately felt like an idiot. How could I have missed that name? Of course I knew who he was. Every agent knew — or should know — that name. We learned about all attempted and successful attempts on protectee's lives. How in the world did I need an introduction? When he had gotten to me, I was a bit overwhelmed. The first thing that went through my mind was *He should have been carrying that casket, not me.* I was not worthy of that honor. When it was time to work, he did what he was trained to do.

There was no detection of ego in his demeanor toward us, and after everyone had purchased a coffee and chitchatted, I knew the day was one I would never forget.

I've sometimes joked that agents are merely bullet sponges or expendable human shields. That's all we're good for as we stood by for that moment when we wouldn't react out of natural human instinct. Instead of ducking for cover at the sound or view of an attack, agents throw themselves in harm's way as if it's a natural reaction, making themselves as big as possible to block whatever is headed their way. But it's not a joking matter at all, and Mr. McCarthy knows that better than anybody.

The day of the official memorial service was less hectic than I'd imagined it would be. A giant tent was built for the thousand-plus invited attendees. Mrs. R.'s casket was placed on the stage, the white roses standing out as even more beautiful. With so many protectees attending, the agents working those advances were busier than I was. My post would be at the back of the room where the press riser was built.

When it was time, I took my post and noted the many familiar faces from the local news channels getting their notes, cameras, and perfectly spackled faces ready for the event. The attendees filed in peacefully, a fast-walking Secret Service suit occasionally scurrying to his or her place as the other protectees began arriving. At one point, I looked slightly to my right and saw the current Secret Service Director Joseph Clancy in the doorway.

The ceremony started, and in poetic fashion it started to rain. There was music and thoughtful speeches, mostly full of funny quips and stories about Mrs. Reagan. Patty Davis, Mrs. Reagan's daughter, spoke. I saw her regularly at the house. She spoke about choosing to remember the good times as opposed to the bad times, hinting at a troubled relationship with her mother.

I had judged Patty too harshly, making comments in the command post about how she only visited her mother for less than thirty minutes each week even though she lived close by. I judged her for not being at her mother's side when she passed. I was full of criticism until I heard her speak. Mrs. R. was far from a perfect mother. That much should be a given since no parent is ever perfect. But Patty clearly had a tumultuous relationship with her mom, and who was I to judge how she grieved and processed this loss? Who was I to make assumptions about the state of her heart? I had felt terrible as she spoke, and I hurt for her.

Well-known newscaster Tom Brokaw spoke about Mrs. R.'s support and protection of her husband, citing an instance when he had said something about Ronald Reagan that Mrs. R. found distasteful. She had no trouble giving the cold shoulder to someone who spoke ill of her husband. She was fiercely protective of him, and I loved those stories. I loved how much she loved him. I knew versions of some of those stories in a very general sense but not from the actual sources. It felt in some small way as if she was finally coming to life to me.

For the first time, I began to understand her and like her more than fear her. I'd been witness to arguably one her most personal moments at the end of her life in the funeral home, but I had no idea who this woman really was, specifically as a wife.

I related to her in that I was always fiercely defensive of Steve while we were married, never (or rarely) saying a bad word about him in public despite everything. I was his cheerleader even when he wasn't around, defending his lack of employment or whatever it was I felt needed defending. Steve sometimes referred to me as a mama bear. Mess with my people, and I'll bite your head off.

When former Canadian Prime Minister Brian Mulroney took the podium, my emotions nearly got the better of me. He spoke mostly of Ronald Reagan's love for his wife. He recalled an instance when both men were together and caught glimpses of their wives, both commenting on how lucky they were. He referenced the letters Ronald Reagan wrote to Mrs. Reagan, regular letters meant for her eyes only. I had heard of those letters during the past week when a longtime staff member told me Mrs. Reagan kept every single note, letter, and telegram in a bag. But until that point, I hadn't read any of them.

Mr. Mulroney read one particular letter aloud that day at the library. It was written on the Reagan's first Christmas in the White House, December 25, 1981.

Dear Mrs. R,

I still don't feel right about you opening an envelope instead of a gift package.

There are several much beloved women in my life and on Christmas, I should be giving them gold, precious stones, perfume, furs and lace. I know that even the best of these would still fall far short of expressing how much these several women mean to me and how empty my life would be without them.

There is of course my 'First Lady.' She brings so much grace and charm to whatever she does that even stuffy, formal functions sparkle and turn into fun times. Everything is done with class. All I have to do is wash up and show up.

There is another woman in my life who does things I don't always get to see but I do hear about them and sometimes see photos of her doing them. She takes an abandoned child in her arms on a hospital visit. The look on her face only the Madonna could match. The look on the child's face is one of adoration. I know because I adore her too.

She bends over a wheelchair or bed to touch an elderly invalid with tenderness and compassion just as she fills my life with warmth and love.

There is another gal I love who is a nest builder. If she was stuck three days in a hotel room, she'd manage to make it home sweet home. She moves things around—looks at it—straightens this and that and you wonder why it wasn't that way in the first place.

I'm also crazy about the girl who goes to the ranch with me. If we're tidying up the woods, she's a peewee power house at pushing over dead trees. She's a wonderful person to sit by the fire with, or to ride with or first to be with when the sun goes down or the stars come out. If she ever stopped going to the ranch, I'd stop too because I'd see her in every beauty spot there is, and I couldn't stand that.

Then there is a sentimental lady I love whose eyes fill up so easily. On the other hand she loves to laugh, and her laugh is like tinkling bells. I hear those bells and feel good all over even if I tell a joke she's heard before.

Fortunately, all these women in my life are you—fortunately for me that is, for there could be no life for me without you. Browning asked: "How do I love thee? Let me count the ways." For there is no way to count. I love the whole gang of you—Mommie, first lady, the sentimental you, the fun you, and the peewee power house of you.

And oh yes, one other very special you—the little girl who takes a "nana" to bed in case she gets hungry in the night. I couldn't and don't sleep well if she isn't there—so please always be there.

Merry Christmas you all—with all my love.

Lucky me.

While he read, I struggled to hold back the tears. I envied that love. I wanted that love. How beautiful it was for Ronald Reagan to write his wife a letter every time they were apart and sometimes just because. There were no social media sites to flaunt his kind gestures. There was no other intended audience except for the woman he loved. I later learned some of the letters were written when they were quarreling. Yet he still wrote to her anyway.

I'll never know the inner workings of their lives and marriage, but I'm certain it's fair to say that regardless of political opinions, there was no doubt Nancy Reagan was loved tremendously and was safely able to love equally as hard in return.

That realization was a confirmation of sorts. My failed marriage had been failing from the beginning, a union fraught with uneven effort and withheld love due to resentment at the first sign of difficulty. I thought about one of Steve's final statements to me: "I'm sorry I can't love you the way you need to be loved."

I loved how safely Mrs. R. was free to love and be loved in return. Maybe Ronald Reagan had gotten it wrong once in a previously failed relationship, but he'd told her in a letter that he didn't care that it took so long to find her because the finding was that much sweeter. He would never reject her, and she knew it. I wanted that.

I turned my body slightly away so the press wouldn't be able to see me tearing up, and I pulled myself together by taking a deep breath and turned my focus to the crowd as the service went on.

Nancy's son, Ron, also spoke at the funeral. During his remarks, he said, "If my mother had one great talent, I think it was that she knew how to love."

Mrs. Reagan left a legacy of love. Despite all scandals, political opinions, and strained relationships, all anyone talked about was Mrs. Reagan's huge capacity to love. I thought I knew how to love, but I suspected I really didn't have a clue. But I knew one thing: I wanted to love like she loved.

When the service was over, people began filing out. The crowd eventually dispersed, and the rain continued drizzling. Allison Borio, another longtime Reagan staff member, came up to me while everyone was leaving. She said she heard I'd been the one to monitor a majority of the embalming and body preparations for Mrs. Reagan.

"That must have been really hard," she said and looked at me sympathetically.

That draining day suddenly began to feel very long. I was ready for the shift to be over. But we weren't done yet. As our supervisor had said earlier that week, we would protect her until she was laid to rest.

There were tractors, floodlights, and workers outside at the mausoleum where Ronald Reagan was buried and where Mrs. Reagan would be buried that night. It was getting dark, and I was cold, shivering outside as the workers dug and pried the mausoleum open. It was an eerie sound when the giant slab creaked open, one that made me feel like I was intruding on an intimate moment. I couldn't see into the opening because it was dark, but I knew Ronald Reagan's remains were in there. The crane slowly lowered the giant box Mrs. R.'s casket was now encased in, the sound of the machines masking the somber aura around the large hole.

I witnessed the moment Mr. and Mrs. Reagan were physically together again. It seemed so final. At least now she could rest in peace next to her Ronnie.

When the workers closed the mausoleum and filled the large hole again, our Assistant to the Special Agent in Charge (ATSAIC) told us we were done. The floodlights and the machines were in full force as I started walking back to the library to gather my things from the security office.

Someone got pizza for us. It's funny that I remember the pizza because it seems so minuscule and irrelevant on the surface, but I remember that piece of pizza tasting so delicious. For someone with food issues, finding something delicious was rare. At the Reagan Library that rainy night, scarfing a piece of pizza with a handful of agents encircling a pizza box was a brief and helpful pause. The taste of combination pizza (the ones with olives and bell peppers and onions) brings me back to that moment even to this day. I can see our faces, but we didn't talk about anything except our growling stomachs and my blue lips and cold white hands.

I fell apart as I drove home. The release was cleansing, my fatigue sidelined by sadness and a dreaded sense of pending doom. Now that this was over, it was time for me to await my fate with the agency, a fate I already knew but hadn't become official yet.

The wait was short. My confirmation came the following Monday. I was being transferred to Washington DC effective July 24, 2016.

CHAPTER 20

NEEDS OF
THE SERVICE

THE DAYS AND WEEKS AFTER the funeral were hectic. Most of us on the Reagan detail were pimped out for 2016 Presidential Campaign travel. The Reagan Operations Office in Westwood began the process of shutting down, and mountains of paperwork and documents filled the halls as the detail would officially cease to exist in a few weeks after everything had been accounted for.

I couldn't get the funeral or the Reagans out of my mind. I wanted to know more about their relationship and how they had made it work with the crazy schedules and a spotlight life. I wanted something I didn't have, asking myself over and over again, "Where did I go wrong? What was their secret?"

But more pressing matters needed my immediate attention. All the divorce paperwork had been turned in to the courts, but I was still waiting to get the documents back with a judge's signature. Nothing was final yet.

My transfer orders indicated I was to report to the Dignitary

Protective Division (DPD) on July 24, 2016. DPD is a division responsible for protecting traveling dignitaries to the DC area or in the field if a local field office can't provide all the manpower. Most agents transferring to DC for a permanent protection detail started in DPD before being assigned to either the Presidential Protective Division (PPD) or Vice Presidential Protective Division (VPD).

Also, when agents received a Permanent Change of Station (PCS) transfer like I did, they typically had 120 days to report to their new assignment. There were options to report a little earlier or a little later, but there were limits to these changes. For example, if an agent's report date was in October, they may request to report in September because they had children who would need to start school. Or if an agent's home sold quickly and escrow closed two weeks before his/her report date, the agent may request to report earlier because it was most convenient. There was a little flexibility to accommodate normal life circumstances associated with a big move.

All new agents sign a Mobility Agreement. By signing, I acknowledged the possibility and likelihood that I would have to relocate while employed, maybe multiple times. A transfer order should have come as no surprise, in other words. But oftentimes it was difficult to estimate or anticipate when a transfer might be coming. Between 2007 and 2016, the typical career track and timeline for agents varied, often at the convenience of headquarters or the "needs of the Service."

Most agents roll their eyes at the phrase "needs of the Service" because it often comes before bad news or an undesirable assignment such as finding out at ten p.m. you're on a five a.m. flight the next morning because someone had a family emergency or additional personnel were needed. The unlucky agent would get a call late at night with the "needs of the Service" line. It was your clue to mentally prepare for a plot twist in your carefully laid plans.

Per my transfer orders, I had two weeks to submit a hardship request memo if I felt I was unable to comply with the transfer. A team of supervisors would review the requests and determine if they were valid or worthy of accommodating when weighed against agency policy and the ever-so-vague case-by-case basis.

I'd been on Nancy Reagan's detail less than a year. The supervisors hardly knew me, and since her detail was an easy assignment, they were never able to see my work ethic like my bosses in Protection Operations or other squads in Los Angeles. The Secret Service's office politics were frustrating, especially if you didn't know someone to make a call for you when you needed someone to put in a good word. It's just the way it was. No one said I had to like it.

I was worried… really worried. I was technically still being treated for depression, and I was technically still married because I didn't have signed divorce papers yet. Regardless of logistics and trivialities, I knew I was in no shape to make a cross-country move. *Why can't I catch a freaking break? Why did Mrs. R. have to die in the middle of the divorce? Why is this happening to me? Am I being punished for all my wrongdoings? This isn't fair.* Yeah, well, news flash: life isn't always fair.

I decided to submit a hardship request. My hardship memo was submitted March 22, 2016. I asked to delay the transfer for one year, citing the divorce and the depression treatment. I knew it was a long shot. Agents have a terribly high divorce rate, and if statistics held true, the supervisors reviewing the document had likely been through one or two themselves.

There were five agents on Mrs. Reagan's detail who received out-of-state transfers. One agent decided to move. She had four kids and couldn't afford to be unemployed. Within a year of transferring, her marriage fell apart. Another agent took an opening on former president Jimmy Carter's detail and moved to Georgia. The three others, including myself, submitted hardship memos.

And then we waited. And waited. Our futures were at the mercy of a handful of supervisors in DC who would likely not be sympathetic to the Reagan Rejects. We didn't get responses until May.

I kept going to counseling with the eating disorder specialist. I was counting down the days to ask the psychiatrist if I could try weaning off the meds. I just wanted that whole phase of my life to be over. I wanted to move on and be happy and leave the mess behind me.

April 2016 was a difficult month. Despite asking my bosses several times if they'd heard anything about my hardship memo being reviewed, there was never any update. Silence. No news was definitely not good news. April was also the month Steve and I had gotten married. A couple of days before our anniversary, he came over with his brother to get some of his things out of the garage. He wasn't nice that day, and I should have just left it alone. Instead, I opened my big mouth.

"Maybe you could not be a jerk this week of all weeks."

"What's different about this week?" he said with a look of disgust.

"Our anniversary, you asshole."

He didn't say anything. He just walked out of the house. The anniversary came and went. We didn't communicate at all that day.

Finally, on May 3, 2016, I received a response from DC about my hardship memo.

"…although the Hardship Committee is sympathetic to your situation, your request was not approved." — US Secret Service, Decision on Hardship Request, dated May 3, 2016

I'm not going to bash the Secret Service because I'm angry they wouldn't accommodate me when I wanted to delay the move. I'm well aware my hardship request didn't have a leg to stand on per policy standards. However, I know I probably would have stayed on the job if the request had been granted. It would have been a win-win situation for everyone involved.

I would've been a much-needed, able-bodied agent working

the campaign trail during an exceptionally busy year in an exceptionally busy field office like Los Angeles. I even quoted Director Clancy's congressional testimony in my memo when he spoke of the agency's attrition problems.

One Reagan detail agent with transfer orders had a daughter who'd been receiving cancer treatments for years. When it was his time to go to Phase 2 (Protection Phase), he chose the Reagan detail because his daughter's doctors were nearby. It didn't make him a bad agent because he wasn't. His hardship request was denied because "comparable care" was available in DC. He moved to DC.

Another agent filed a hardship memo due to child custody issues. His wife was unable to leave California due to custody agreements from another relationship. His request was conditionally approved, but in 2017 it was denied and he had to leave the job.

I felt stuck between a rock and a hard place because, after all, I was a single and independent woman. I had to have a job. No one else was going to take care of me, and I'm not the type to allow it.

I went to DC for a temporary assignment around that time. It was awful in a cutthroat, disgruntled kind of way. I met my friend Brit at the Washington Field Office. Brit's one of the kindest women I know, but she was the exception in that office. No one said hello to each other. It was an every-man-for-himself vibe.

Agents in DC were worked to the bone, and I suspected the senior agent's attitudes had started to rub off on the new hires, making the newbies disgruntled and cocky before they even got their feet wet. My life had enough negativity already. I left that assignment with a sinking feeling: *I can't go to DC right now.*

I also got a call from the lead Secret Service Rescue Swimmers asking if I wanted to be an instructor for the course that June. It was a glimmer of happiness for me. I was still swimming and going to Krav Maga, so I was in shape. I went to my Reagan supervisors and probably looked like a sad puppy dog as I said, "It would mean so much to me if you said yes. Please?" Thankfully, they did.

Final divorce papers came with the judge's signatures. I talked to a Realtor, and we made plans to put the house on the market in June while I was out of town.

All those little decisions solidified one thing: after nine years with an agency I'd devoted my life to, I was not going to leave at twenty-five years and a retirement party. I had planned to keep working and turn in my notice two weeks before my DC report date. I'd made the decision, but I was far from at peace about it. *When am I going to wake up from this bad dream?*

I arrived at Beltsville in early June and breathed in the chlorine at the training tank with a smile on my face. It felt so good to be back. Colin, the former Division I swimmer in my 2012 rescue swimmer class, had since transferred to President Obama's detail and was also an instructor.

My house went on the market, and it was in escrow within just a couple of days. My beloved house — the one I loved so much and took pride in owning — was not going to be mine for much longer. I was going to make enough money on the house to have a little cushion when I left the job the following month. Maybe it was the chlorine in my veins making me so optimistic, but I decided I needed to take some time off. I was being given a gift, an opportunity many never get. I had a chance to quit my job after a divorce and some circumstances outside my control. I had time to heal. That much I could look forward to, and I was thankful.

I got to jump out of the helicopter one last time with the Coast Guard. The roar of the engines and the rotor wash stinging my arms and face brought back the same smile as it did the first time I jumped. As I looked up at the helicopter above me and the boat a short distance away, I felt a bittersweet happiness.

When I got back to Los Angeles, I needed to find a place to move and fast. I quickly figured out that affordable rent in Los

Angeles was hard to come by, and if a place became available, it was gone within hours of listing. I found a place in West Los Angeles but only after applying and getting approved prior to even seeing it. My escrow on the house was scheduled to close in early July, but the buyers were investors and agreed to a rent-back for a short time if I had any problems finding a place right away.

In the meantime, I had to start going through years of stuff in the house, and all my stuff seemed to involve Steve. He'd taken a lot of our things, but many photos and reminders remained. Since I was downsizing from a three-bedroom house to a one-bedroom apartment, I decided to start fresh and get rid of anything that didn't have sentimental value. It was freeing. Craigslist buyers swept up much of it, and the local Goodwill knew my face after a couple of trunks full of memories were dropped off.

I showed up to work and kept trying not to be sad as the days ticked by. I had my resignation notification drafted. It was just a waiting game by that point.

Steve sent me an email the day the divorce was final at the end of June. He said he didn't deserve me and that he'd never find another Mel. He told me to go find someone who would love me and deserve me. He said he'd be there for me if I ever needed something in a pinch, but I knew it wasn't true. He asked to be friends or at least check in on each other.

I sent a response, but it was curt. I said we couldn't be friends and that I wouldn't check in with him so he knew I was okay. I said I wouldn't keep the dogs from him and that he was free to see them anytime.

I hit the Send button and sighed. *You just became like all the rest, Steve. You think this is supposed to make me feel better? All it means is that I wasn't worth it to you. It was easier to let me go than love me at my worst. I stood by you. I only wanted you. Don't you get that? At the end of the day, I still wanted you.*

CHAPTER 21

A COMPLICATED RESIGNATION

DECIDING TO QUIT MY JOB without another one lined up was probably the most uncharacteristic choice I've ever made to date. In any other circumstance, quitting would not have been an option. As July 2016 rolled around, I would catch myself in the mirror and whisper, "What are you doing, Mel? What's gotten into you?"

Trauma is a word often avoided in the law-enforcement community, especially when referring to a difficult shift or a difficult situation. I bristled when my therapist referred to some of my experiences as traumatic. Child-porn cases, divorce, Mrs. Reagan's embalming, et cetera. They were all deemed traumatic. I laughed at her once. How could my experiences be traumatic? I wasn't a combat veteran who saw terrible things and came home with post-traumatic stress. I wasn't my ex-husband who had to respond to calls of teenage suicide or a drowned toddler. I'd never witnessed a terrorist attack firsthand. I'd never been kidnapped and sold into sex slavery. Those things are traumatic.

I just had a lot going on in my personal life, and I was getting help.

"I'm fine." Always just freaking fine.

A little wrench had gotten thrown into my resignation plan though. The Secret Service had what's called a "leave restriction" in place the week before my transfer date. The Republican National Convention (RNC) would be taking place in Cleveland, Ohio, that week, and the conventions are an all-hands-on-deck kind of experience like the annual United Nations General Assembly in New York every fall. In other words, don't take a vacation during a leave restriction.

I submitted a leave request for that final week anyway. I would be able to get keys to my apartment before the convention, and the less rent-back time I took from the house buyers the better. My supervisor knew I was going to be leaving the job, so I had hoped that he would get permission to approve my leave. After all, I had over two hundred hours of vacation time I'd never taken. That was wishful thinking though, and the request was denied. Therefore, I had to resign one week earlier to avoid being on the road when I needed to be out of the house. *Good Lord, this just can't go smoothly, can it?*

I asked the psychiatrist if I could start weaning off the meds. I was relieved when she agreed. I wanted to move on with my life even though the unknown was frightening. I wanted to prove to myself that my depression diagnosis was situational and circumstantial as opposed to a chronic condition. I really didn't want that diagnosis to follow me forever.

I started weaning off the meds per the doctor's recommendations.

Then things got complicated. I turned in my resignation as planned with the resignation date bumped back to avoid the RNC leave restriction. But just as I was adjusting to the idea of being unemployed, I got a call about a position in the Los Angeles Field Office as an Investigative Analyst. It was a full-time position at my current pay grade. I wouldn't be an agent anymore, but I'd have a full-time job, something I knew I responsibly needed to pursue. I went through the interviews, researched the position, and made sure it was something I could do successfully.

However, I couldn't resign as an agent because that would make me ineligible for the new position since it was only open to current government employees. I wrote a painful email to my boss saying I had changed my mind about quitting due to applying for the alternative position. (Queue more complicated circumstances.)

Within hours of rescinding my resignation, I received an assignment at the RNC in Cleveland, Ohio. I constantly asked my boss if he'd heard anything about the new position. Anything. Any update at all. Nothing. I waited and waited for any inkling of my fate, yet not one word. Crickets. The days crept by without one single update.

I flew to Cleveland for my RNC assignment feeling absolutely terrible. Apparently, I could be quite indecisive as I adjusted to this new reality as a single woman. I didn't have a partner to consider. My decisions really only affected me at that point, and it was entirely unfamiliar territory. I wanted clarity. I wanted someone to tell me what to do.

Despite the spectacle of election years, my assignment at the RNC was humdrum. I was one of the agents escorting the media buses from their staging area to the convention venue. It was a five-minute ride through a heavily guarded, gated area. Since everything had to be cleared by bomb technicians and K-9s, equipment could not be left unattended, hence my presence on the buses to ensure everything and everyone stayed clean.

All day long, back and forth I went, listening to griping about any delays due to motorcade movements or demonstrations.

"I'm live in five minutes. What's the holdup?" I heard it at least ten times per day, and I ignored a couple of awkward remarks from passengers.

One cameraman said, "Hey, does the Secret Service have a sexy calendar like firemen? Because if you're in it, I'd buy one." Each time we'd pass a sweaty coworker posted along the route, I'd remind myself to appreciate this luxurious and rare post in air-conditioned buses.

During the RNC, Secret Service personnel were housed at area university dorms, likely because the local hotels were sold out or ridiculously expensive. My room looked like any typical dorm, complete with the staples of basic college living: community bathroom, twin-size bed, desk, mini fridge, and microwave.

I woke up with a start the morning of July fifteenth, the scratchy sheets crinkling like paper at the disturbance.

"I have to quit," I said aloud with certainty. My hand came to my mouth, shocked at the sudden conviction. But I just knew.

I've been known to ignore my intuition because I didn't like what it was saying. Intuition can be funny that way. I've often assumed my intuition needed the corrective lenses of my internal justifications and reasoning. In other words, I've been known to make excuses for bad decisions. But I knew the truth or best move all along; I just chose to twist it to accommodate the latest insecurity, fear, or someone else's wishes.

With my hands still on my mouth, I started to chuckle. I looked around the college dorm room and thought of myself as a seventeen-year-old girl moving into her first dorm room fourteen years prior. I was clueless and insecure as my roommate, and I decorated our room with those old Abercrombie & Fitch bags with hot guys on them, the ones you could cut out into a poster. We regularly watched *Coyote Ugly* — my favorite movie at the time — as I stressed about silly general education classes. How ironic it was to make a gutsy decision with surety in a college environment, an environment where I had once previously been fraught with self-doubt.

I was assigned the afternoon shift at the RNC, and we were picked up by giant buses every day to drive to Cleveland. I walked to the cafeteria area for a snack before I notified my boss, delaying and procrastinating just to be sure I was really certain about resigning for good. But there was no need to delay. I sent my boss my final resignation before my shift. I told him I was taking control of my life, and I would not be reporting to Washington DC after the convention. I would not wait any longer for someone to get around to updating me about the Investigative Analyst position.

I felt sad, but that sadness was overcome with relief when my boss responded. He wrote, "Just go be happy. We'll figure out the rest." The rest would be logistics, turning in my gear, notifying everyone, et cetera, but I didn't worry about that right then.

I couldn't believe I'd done it. Was I crazy or brave? That much I didn't know yet. I was too busy mentally preparing for the flinch-inducing consequences if this turned out badly.

All I had to do was finish my assignment in Cleveland. Despite the relief, I knew I needed to watch my tongue for the next few days. Sometimes tact and class, while quieter than anger and frustration, are the best qualities to take to the exit door. I reminded myself of this each morning as I adorned my suit and gear.

People asked me a lot of questions during that last week. I couldn't help it. My stupid RNC credential had Reagan Protective Division (RPD) plastered under my name. Everyone wanted to know the fate of the RPD agents. I made every effort to stick to the facts, yet I'm sure people read through the lines. We all worked for the same agency. We knew about the problems and issues plaguing agency morale. I was angry, and many would agree it was justified. The fact that it took so long for a couple of supervisors to review a hardship memo was really unacceptable. The fact that I hadn't heard a single peep about the analyst position wasn't right. How could they let it go so long without notifying me of *anything?*

I think they were calling my bluff. I think they thought I'd desperately report to DC because I needed a job just like most other people. They were wrong.

I'm glad I didn't walk out of the RNC with two middle fingers pointed at the Secret Service. At the end of the day, how I acted mattered. That much the divorce had taught me. Sometimes airing beefs in rants and raves delegitimizes the beefs when they're expressed in excessively emotional ways.

The night the RNC concluded, I walked to the command post for my suitcase. One of the RNC site agents from the Los Angeles Field Office was coming out as I was walking in.

"Hey Mel, are you going to send an email with your contact information to everyone so we can keep in touch with you?"

I had already sent an email, but I didn't send it to everyone. I sent it to everyone on RPD, my training class, and a handful of close friends. The site agent was a cool guy, but I hadn't included him. I guess I didn't know he would have wanted to be included, and I felt bad. I knew his girlfriend who was also an agent, and I had included her.

All I could muster was, "I sent an email already. Um… your girlfriend has my info." Ouch.

He just walked away without a word. If my shoulders could have slumped any more, they would have. *Dude, I just finished my last shift ever. Please cut me some slack. Please don't just walk away.*

While everyone went back to the dorms to pack for the Democratic National Convention, I caught an Uber to the airport. I looked at my badge and my agent lapel pin, knowing it would be the last time I'd wear them.

The driver pulled up and said, "Hey, you Mel?"

"Yeah," I said and climbed into the car.

"Were you at the convention this week?"

"Yeah, I'm glad it's over."

"Same. Traffic has been terrible this week. So many road

closures." He looked at me from the rearview mirror, and I nodded. He stopped talking then, and I was grateful.

After I flew home from the RNC, I still had to return my issued gear to the Los Angeles Field Office. The following week, I met with my RPD supervisor and a Special Officer to do my property inventory and final debrief. We sat in an office, checking serial numbers and ensuring everything was accounted for including my gun, badge, credentials, ballistic vest, baton, radio, et cetera.

"Good luck to you, Mel." Those were my supervisor's last words when all was accounted for. I was a little hurt. I was hoping for "I'm sorry you're leaving. We are losing a good agent. We wish you'd reconsider."

On the other hand, I suppose I needed a bit of luck since I was officially unemployed as of that moment.

I walked to the elevator landing, feeling naked and light without the gun and annoying government cell that buzzed constantly. It was the first time in nine years that I didn't have both with me. As I waited for the elevator, a man walked up. I didn't know him, but that wasn't unusual in a larger office like Los Angeles.

"Hey," he said pleasantly. "Are you one of the new agents? I haven't seen you yet."

It hit me like a freight train: I'd already been replaced. Already forgotten. My job had been my identity for nearly a decade. Now it suddenly wasn't.

I rushed out of the building, desperate to get to my car without seeing anyone I knew. I was climbing the steps outside the Ernst and Young Building that led to the Target parking garage where my car was parked, and the tears started to come. I looked up and saw an LAPD Detective coming down the stairs toward me. She and I had shared an office in ECTF for a time, and she had always been kind to me.

I'd been ignoring her for a while because I knew she'd force an honest conversation out of me. She had a way of reading me and knowing when I was not okay. I'd been isolating myself from most people anyway. That's what I tended to do when I was struggling. But this time I was so grateful she was there.

"Melon," she said, shocked to see me. I never had the heart to tell her my name was not Melon like a cantaloupe or watermelon, but her sweet heart was larger than any melon anyway.

"I just turned in all my gear, and I don't know what I'm going to do. I just quit my job."

She walked me toward my car, hugging me and saying, "It's going to be okay." That's probably exactly what I needed to hear.

I sobbed and sobbed in my car, unable to drive and consumed with sadness. It was the end of an era. But I was not a quitter. I was just getting started. But what was I starting exactly?

CHAPTER 22

CRASHING WITH
THE DOGS

PEOPLE TALK ABOUT CRASHING, THAT feeling after being strong for a while and finally having to face what happened. I'd been so busy making changes and dealing with logistical circumstances that I had an excuse for leaving the emotional ramifications unaddressed. I no longer had that excuse, and the loneliness came crashing down hard like that one poorly timed wave when you're swimming past the break. I went tumbling around searching for the surface. I had been alone for several months by then, but I finally had to face it head-on. I wasn't sure I liked being in my own company.

My new apartment was in an old, small building in West Los Angeles. My unit had been newly remodeled, so the walls were bright white and the floors covered in cheap laminate wood-ish flooring. It had one bedroom, and everything was visible except for the bathroom by standing just inside the front door. It was perfect. I never understood why people on those house-hunting-type shows wanted large bedrooms in their large houses.

Bedrooms are for sleeping and sex usually, and neither requires a ton of space. But that's just me. I didn't (and still don't) have a lot of stuff. Going from chaotic to simple gave me a sense of order, I suppose.

The dull yet bright space was quickly made brighter by all types of colors. My bedspread looked like Bohemian and Moroccan décor had a vibrant baby. I made a table covered in pennies and built from galvanized piping from the hardware store. Vases of fake flowers I bought at Goodwill sat on counters, and my walls were covered in random eclectic artwork and family photos. There wasn't much furniture in the place, but what was there was cheap, secondhand, and decorated with color. It was a positive-looking apartment by the time I'd spent my first night there.

I didn't have much help moving, and even though I'd sold most of the heavy stuff, I struggled with moving what I had kept. I didn't really ask anyone for help. I think I just needed to prove to myself that I didn't need anybody.

I was very sore after I had gotten everything inside the apartment and decorated, but I felt like I should have been feeling positive by that point. *Everyone keeps saying things will get better. When is that going to start happening?* After all, those main stressors were officially gone. Dealing with the Secret Service was no longer a source of stress. I wasn't feeling stuck in an unhappy marriage. I had the luxury of free time as well as the luxury of financial freedom to take some time off.

But I crashed on July 31, 2016. It was my second night in the new apartment. The sting of rejection hit harder than it had all those months before. I didn't have an excuse to avoid dealing with it. There was literally nothing to do except walk the dogs, feed the dogs, and, well, figure out what to do with the influx of free time. I had too much time to think, and I thought myself into a dark, lonely place.

I'd thought about suicide after the Dark Night with Steve, but those thoughts scared me and were quickly dismissed. But that night I looked at it differently.

I'm alone. My sister has a new baby. My parents live out of state, and I don't want them to worry any more than they already are. All my friends are agents. They're traveling and don't have free time to hang out with me. I can't leave my apartment for more than a couple of hours because these poor dogs have never lived in an apartment.

I don't want to be alone. Maybe this is the end of the line for me. Nobody wants me. I'm not worth anyone's time. It's like I'm one big energy drain. I'd rather die than be alone for the rest of my life. And that's what I'm going to be. I'm just a pile of baggage that has no meaning in her life. I just want this sadness to stop. I can't take it anymore.

Those thoughts started on the cheap futon I had in the living room and got darker by the minute. I didn't want my death to be messy, so the idea of using a gun was out of the question. I knew I wouldn't slit my wrists because I don't like knives.

Eventually I wandered into the bathroom. I looked at myself in the mirror. I looked older. I wasn't young and full of life anymore. But mostly, I just looked tired. I opened the cabinet to find a tissue, and I saw all the bottles. I'd weaned myself off the antidepressants, but I still had two bottles in the cabinet. I don't know if downing two months' worth of antidepressants would've killed me, but in that moment, it seemed like the most peaceful option. I even had a bottle of an over-the-counter sleep aid and miscellaneous bottles of ibuprofen and other headache pain relievers to allegedly help with this peaceful end.

Maybe someone would find me like the singer Amy Winehouse. Despite the turmoil of her lifestyle, Amy passed away in her sleep and was described as peaceful when she was found. Maybe people would say the same of me. It wouldn't be fair to leave a gruesome scene. *That would just be selfish.*

Eventually I brought all the bottles into the kitchen area, but instead of opening them, I slid down onto the floor and stared blankly at the cabinet in front of me. When the marriage was ending, I would cry so hard in the shower that I would throw up and dry heave. It all started again on the apartment's kitchen floor… the crying and the coughing. Rejection.

I'm not okay.

For several minutes I just cried, blurrily looking up at the bottles on the counter before pulling my knees to my chest again. I got up at one point and filled a water bottle and set all the pill bottles on the floor next to me.

Let's get this over with.

Then something happened.

Anja, my little eighteen-pound Norwegian Lundehund, started whining and yipping softly at me. She came up to me and nudged my elbow with her nose so my arm flopped around her neck. She sat down and continued to whine. I glanced over at her and then saw the other two Chihuahua mixes staring at me, more bug-eyed than normal.

Anja was originally Steve's dog. He'd gotten her as a puppy before we got married. But she had grown very attached to me and became my sidekick. Lundehunds can be a little skittish and look like a fox or a small coyote. She wasn't really a cuddly dog, but she dominated hikes like a champ.

I had Bella before Steve and I got married. She was the top dog of the group. Darla was the newest addition. I went into PetSmart a couple of years prior to this, and a local rescue was there. I saw a skinny, shaking Chihuahua mix staring straight at me.

Don't make eye contact. You don't need another dog.

But, of course, I walked over to her after I bought dog food. The poor thing was so scared. The lady running the adoption area told me Darla was a stray and was found with a puppy. The puppy had been adopted but not her. I knelt down to pick her up, and she cowered. I lifted her up and held her close.

I don't think Steve really wanted Darla. A year or two before we got her, Steve had picked up a stray while he was working. No one claimed the dog, and he wanted to bring him home.

"Steve, we have two dogs already, and they don't get nearly enough attention as it is." I came around, but it was too late. The shelter had already put him down. I felt terrible, and I know Steve was really upset with me about it. I felt guilty coming to him later about another dog.

I was really afraid Steve would take Anja when we split, but she was so attached to me. Thankfully, he didn't want to take the dogs. Whatever his reasons, I didn't care. I didn't want to lose my girls.

Anja kept nudging at me until I brought my knees down into a cross-legged position. She curled up into my lap and wouldn't move. I looked at her furry little body in my lap and realized I couldn't kill myself. It was like she knew I needed to be reminded that I wasn't alone.

People say I love my dogs too much. "They're just dogs," they say. I struggled with three in a one-bedroom apartment. They barked at the new noises, and they weren't used to being on the leashes every time they went outside. Anja struggled more than the others. I trained her to run off-leash, and the first couple of days on those Los Angeles streets were rough. I had to drag her a couple of times, and she just didn't want to be on a leash. We were all adjusting to this new life.

But in that moment, Anja was like an angel. She showed me love when I felt most unlovable. She reminded me that I wasn't alone. She didn't reject me even though I hadn't been very patient with her while we were adjusting to this new life.

It's hard to think about that night because I usually wonder what would have happened had Anja not climbed into my lap. How long would it have taken for someone to find me? Those poor dogs would have been so scared. They'd run out of food and water. I knew I couldn't go through with it... not like that.

When I'd finally picked myself up off the floor, all three followed me around the apartment until I decided to just go to bed and try to deal with life again tomorrow. Anja slept right next to me the entire night, something she didn't usually do. I was not okay, but I wasn't getting my stomach pumped (or worse) in a hospital… and my dog refused to leave my side.

I flushed the pills down the toilet the next morning.

CHAPTER 23

LISTENING TO NANCY REAGAN

THE DOGS GOT ME OUT of bed the next morning and mornings after that. Anja was always the first one to get me up. Bella and Darla were quick to curl up in my lap as I drank coffee or tea and tried to pep talk my way into getting dressed. Anja spinning excitedly when I said the word *walk* brought a smile to my face. I took them to the local dog park, and sometimes we hiked at Loyola Marymount University.

But just because I got dressed and got out of the apartment didn't mean I wasn't isolating myself. Some days I would give myself these arbitrary deadlines.

If I'm not happy at thirty-five, then I'll end it all. No, wait. But what about the dogs? Once the dogs are gone. Then I'll do it if I'm not happy.

I stopped going to Krav Maga classes. But I walked miles and miles every day. I got into a weird groove of walking everywhere. I walked the dogs in the morning, walked three miles to get my mail at an off-site mailbox business around lunchtime, and walked the dogs in the evening again.

Sometimes I would walk to Trader Joe's or The Grove just to walk. I loved walking. I hated my old work commute, and I was grateful to live where I didn't have to drive every day.

I didn't cook. That was something I'd grown to loathe over the years. I cooked almost every night when Steve and I were together. It was yet another thing I resented because the household duties like cleaning, laundry, and cooking, were never equally distributed in our relationship. It was the most frequent argument starter, usually ending with me screaming, "When are you going to realize I'm not the Energizer Bunny?"

"You know what? The more you ask me to do things for you, the more I don't want to do it," he once said.

Instead of cooking, I walked to Vons for premade salad mixes and things like that. I also realized there were certain foods I liked. I was able to have a preference now that I was alone, and I had no idea what I liked anymore.

I came across Jerusalem bagels at this little place called Bibi's when I was walking to get my mail right after I had moved. It became a regular stop for me.

Nights, on the other hand, were exceptionally difficult. I never had problems sleeping in my life. I was usually chronically tired. But I just couldn't sleep in the apartment. It's like I was keeping myself busy during the day so I didn't have to think too much about feeling lonely. Instead of doing something constructive with the insomnia, I binge-watched shows on Netflix and Amazon because I didn't get cable when I moved into the apartment. I'd often see three or four a.m. before I'd pass out just to be woken up a couple of hours later by the dogs. Each day turned into déjà vu. I was surviving, but I definitely wasn't thriving. I'm not sure I would call it healing either.

I ordered the book *I Love You, Ronnie: The Letters of Ronald Reagan to Nancy Reagan.* Those late nights left me plenty of time to ponder and lament my past, including the funeral. I really loved the letter former Canadian Prime Minister Mulroney read. I pored through the book of letters, loving every single minute of the book, even dog-earing and highlighting some of Mrs. Reagan's narrative pages as if it were a textbook. It felt like reading a fairy tale, and I was the little girl in a princess costume watching Cinderella. But this was real.

I was fascinated with the letters because I am a letter writer, a chronic sneaker of little notes into suitcases and lunch boxes. I select birthday cards with care and take the time to actually say something nice or funny, depending on the person. If someone visits me, I will probably sneak a little note into a suitcase or purse for them to find later. I also tend to keep notes and cards given to me. Hearing that Mrs. R. kept all of Ronald Reagan's letters was so cute to me. If I'd received letters like those, I'd cherish each one as she did.

I once took a screenshot of a text Steve sent me years prior. I read it over and over again back then, feeling giddy as I did. We used to joke that he loved his truck more than me, and we referred to the truck as his girlfriend.

Here's what he wrote in the text:

> "Let's look at it this way. My girlfriend is like a Honda Civic, a dime a dozen with lots of money that made it look pretty. You can work on a Civic and make it fast and cool-looking, but in the end it's still a Civic. You, my love, are like a Bel Air. It started life a classic, beautiful and elegant. Even in their old age they are still highly coveted. You, my love, are a Bel Air! The thing every guy wants but some can't have. So he settled for the Civic that he got easy but really doesn't want. Romance in car language [sic]."

When things ended, we kept asking each other, "Where did we go wrong?" For me, it was easier to answer the question, "When did things start to change?"

They say you don't know someone until you see how they respond when something difficult or bad happens. I'm not proud of the behaviors and decisions that followed Steve's job loss in 2008. Resentment was the subtle cancer, the (seemingly) asymptomatic kind that spreads and grows until it's infiltrated the whole relationship, too far gone for treatment to result in enough healing to sustain the structure it used to be.

I made the naive assumption that things would get better once we got married.

That's the stupidest reasoning ever, I remember thinking one late night in the apartment. I'll never admit to being the brightest bulb in the tanning bed when it comes to relationships.

I always felt guilty for researching annulments in 2012. I felt like I was ready to quit, and Lentzes don't quit. I had made the choice to stay and try to get better. But because I'd thought about quitting back then, did that mean I had already quit? Had I just been delaying and patiently waiting for him to give me a reason to lash out or say that something was the last straw? It's sad, but maybe. I had also kept finding reasons to delay parenthood, a classic sign of an unhappy marriage.

Steve grew into the type of cop nobody hears about because of the few bad ones that make the news. Despite our problems, he was a kind and generous person outside the home, even during the tougher years. Hearing about those moments reminded me of the boy at the gas station who didn't feel the need to brag to his girlfriend about helping someone who'd run out of gas.

But at home, he didn't ask how I was, and he didn't express gratitude. Others were getting the best version of him. I was tired of seeing my husband behave like the charming, kind man I fell in love with, but not with me. I blamed him for making me feel undesirable, unwanted, and taken advantage of.

It was a sad and lonely feeling to recognize my entire adult life to that point had involved him. I didn't know adulthood without him, yet he had suddenly become a complete stranger to me. I was comfortable with him, and I believe we stayed together because it was familiar.

On the surface, we were always the happy couple. When people would ask for our marriage advice, I would always say the same thing.

"You're hardest on the people you care about the most. Sometimes you just need to give the other person a break."

That's generally good advice, I think. We expect more from people we give more of ourselves to, and we can forget they're human. But that advice should have some boundaries. Allowing someone to be human is one thing; minimizing and dismissing real issues is another thing entirely. I didn't navigate those boundaries and issues in a healthy way. In the end, I found myself divorced.

As I pondered all this during those long bouts of insomnia in the new apartment, I felt much less anger about my situation. I wanted to break it down and analyze what had happened. Surely there was a magical template for a happy, healthy relationship. Surely something existed to give me answers.

Unfortunately, life doesn't come with a user guide with a tab for RESENTMENT ISSUES IN MARRIAGE with customized answers for my particular situation.

However, Nancy Reagan spoke loudly to me about love and marriage. Once I was quiet enough to recognize the art of silence, she came alive to me. I needed to quiet my anger long enough to listen and learn. I had to turn my focus away from Steve and look inward.

In the book *I Love You, Ronnie,* Nancy Reagan wrote about her marriage, saying, "My life really began when I met Ronald Reagan." She said she was asked for the secret to a happy marriage in a letter written when Reagan was governor of California.

"I wrote back, saying I had no blueprint for marriage, how to make it happy and long-lasting, but that I thought 'mainly you have to be willing to want to give.' Now, as I reflect some more on the life Ronnie and I have shared, I would add that saying how much you love each other – to each other and also in letters that can be saved, read, and reread over the years – is a wonderful way to stay close. It is especially important in our busy lives to keep alive what really matters most: love, caring for each other, finding concrete ways to say it and show it, every

*day and in every way you can. It's what endures, after all, and what
we retain and hold on to, especially in our hearts.*

*One of the things my life has taught me is how important it is to try
to say 'I love you' in ways that can be preserved, looked at and read
when you're alone or when there is adversity or when circumstances
bring separation."*

Sitting on my Craigslist futon with a bagel in my hand, I
realized my loving actions toward Steve were far from loving
even if the actions themselves were generally considered loving.
I told Steve I loved him every day. He did the same. I thought I
was showing him my love by encouraging him and basically
functioning as a mother to him (cleaning the house, laundry,
cooking, packing lunches, et cetera). I'd say those were loving
acts, but over time everything I did for him was done with
resentment. So, was I really demonstrating my love to him daily
and in ways that could be preserved as Nancy said? My
resentment toward Steve eventually overshadowed my love for
him. I loved him more than I could ever describe, but that's a
testament to the magnitude of resentment that was capable of
masking good loving intentions.

There was no going back, and I couldn't change Steve or
make the actions and hurt disappear. But I could make changes
in myself. I could become the version of myself I wanted to be. I
wanted the anger and resentment to leave me forever.

Maybe maturity in a breakup is actually being able to see both
sides, recognize my part, and acknowledge that I can control my
behavior. I was and still am capable of sabotaging my own
growth and healing with the close-minded notion that it takes
two, and therefore, I don't have to take full responsibility for my
actions since I had company.

We were supposed to give each other the best of ourselves,
and we didn't. Other people and jobs got our best. The Secret
Service got my focused attention most days. I should have
ensured that Steve didn't merely get the leftover energy and
kindness I hoped to muster when we were around each other. I

assumed he would understand when circumstances outside our relationship drained me. I used his irresponsibility as an excuse to withhold my best self from my husband. How shameful that realization made me feel.

That realization, however, allowed me to learn from Nancy Reagan's marriage. They thrived together and were able to thrive separately as individuals. The Reagan marriage did not have a sacrificial lamb. There was no jealousy of the other's success or popularity. They knew what they had, and they didn't take it for granted. When he was gone, she continued to thrive because she was a strong woman on her own. Her strength was reinforced by a man who loved her the way she needed to be loved. It's not enough just to feel the love. You have to live it and act it out every single day in resentment-free ways. The Reagans supported each other and allowed the other to shine without fear of being outshined. They were far from perfect, but they made the effort to keep their love at the forefront, leaving little time or reason for resentment to build.

In another letter to a woman asking for marital advice, Mrs. Reagan wrote:

"When two people really love each other[sic] they help each other stay alive and grow."

My preexisting insecurities were magnified because I equated Steve's lack of loving expressions to my lack of deserving love. I thought unhealthy self*less*ness was better than unhealthy narcissism. My own ego put too much pressure on my spouse to make me feel secure. My security rested on his ability to love me just so. That's unfair. I hated so much about myself, and I expected him to fix it with his love. That's different than helping each other stay alive and grow. As spouses, we were supposed to augment our best qualities through love, not fix each other's flaws with love. It sounds straightforward, but anyone who says the implementation of this idea is easy is going to get a giant eye roll from me.

At the beginning of their relationship, the Reagans were actors, the Hollywood types. In *I Love You, Ronnie,* Mrs. R. writes, "Ronnie was always supportive of my work, and he enjoyed my growing success along with me."

I had felt guilty for my success because of Steve's lack of success. But his lack of effort was not my problem to fix. Only he could do that. Where I went wrong was letting his poor behavior affect my ability to take pride in my own accomplishments. Steve always wanted to be a cop, but I didn't always want to be a Secret Service agent. I wasn't confident enough in myself because I was too busy worrying about how my success would make him feel worse about himself. I'd accuse him of making me feel small, but I was really making myself feel small.

At the time, my greatest fear in life was winding up alone. I relied on companionship to validate me. But Nancy Reagan's love story eventually stopped making me feel desperate for companionship. It planted a seed of independence, turning the loneliness of silence and solitude into the art of getting to know myself and who I wanted to be. I'd never been alone in adulthood, and I had no idea who I was or what I really stood for when I found myself in my own company.

Hi, I'm Melanie Lentz. Who am I?

CHAPTER 24

NOT ONE OF THE GIRLS

WHEN I WAS IN PROTECTION Operations in the Los Angeles Field Office, an agent named Josh, a good guy with a Jason Statham-esque vibe, came into our squad's office around lunchtime one day to discuss a protection assignment. He saw me sitting at my desk and said, "Hey, Lentz, how come you're not downstairs with all the girls going to lunch?"

"What lunch?" I didn't know about any lunch. I think he realized he'd put his foot in his mouth because he stammered a bit before answering.

"Oh, I saw them gathering in the lobby." He listed the names of several female agents, administrative assistants, and others he'd seen. They told him they were all headed to lunch together.

"Guess I wasn't invited," I said and looked back at my computer screen, probably poorly masking the flicker of hurt before I turned away.

"Does it bother you that they didn't ask you?"

"Yeah, a little," I replied honestly. "I saw a few of them earlier today at the coffee machine and in the locker room. They had a few opportunities to invite me if they wanted to include me."

Josh chuckled for a second and said something I wasn't expecting.

"Mel, did you really get this job so you could be one of the girls?"

My fingers stopped clicking at the keyboard for a moment. "No, I suppose not," I said as I looked back in his direction. "Thanks for that." That day, I put a three-by-five-inch card on my desk with the words "You did not get this job so you could be one of the girls."

I've never had many female friends. I've typically had a small circle of close friends; and by that, I mean I could count them out on one hand. In college, I seemed to have had more friends around midterms and finals because I took decent notes, a nice asset for the classmates who skipped class and didn't pay attention. I was one of those girls who was insecure enough to allow people to use me because I thought consistent self-sacrifice made me a good person. I just wanted to be normal and accepted, and I never felt normal.

My eating disorder therapist once told me, "Mel, you're a rebel, and you need to be okay with being a rebel. Break the implied rules, and you might find yourself."

I spent a lot of time analyzing, philosophizing, and contemplating the ideas of femininity, modesty, exposure, sexuality, and the women's empowerment movement. The year 2016 was monumental in that regard. Hillary Clinton was the Democratic Party's presidential candidate. Regardless of political affiliation, it was a good year to bring women's issues to a regular topic of conversation.

I went to Miami Beach for a weekend in October 2016. I explored the coastline, got a nice tan, read a book, and relaxed. It was the first time I took a vacation alone.

I walked to the Holocaust Memorial in Miami Beach one evening. On the way back, I stopped for a late dinner at the Aroma Espresso Bar on Collins and Sixteenth.

I hadn't planned on being social that evening. But I wound up talking to a middle-aged woman for over an hour. We talked about all sorts of things, and she got me out of my introverted funk. It was like we'd known each other for years. We talked about our lives and shared our stories and the lessons we'd learned along the way. I told her I was thankful to the Secret Service for making me strong enough to quit and stand up for myself.

"You were always strong enough. You just didn't know it. The Secret Service only showed you," she said.

In actuality, the Secret Service showed me much more than my own strength. Ironically, it taught me about being a woman. I just didn't realize it until I left. Working in a male-dominated and typically masculine environment provided a unique perspective, to be sure. I was given a wealth of knowledge about physical security and protection. I was exposed to things I didn't want to see—namely child pornography—and some things that scared me, like working protective intelligence cases.

I've always been afraid that my life won't matter, that my life would be wasted because I failed to live meaningfully. Never in my wildest dreams would I have thought my experiences in the Secret Service would be subtly preparing me for a meaningful life apart from it.

I had learned about access control, the biggest task within the Secret Service's protective mission. Protecting someone means controlling who gets close. Securing a venue involves plugging holes or access points with agents or law enforcement and funneling everyone through magnetometers at designated access points. It's about creating an environment that's safe for the protectee, one that minimizes the potential for a negative event. Without efficient access control, the protectee's safety is just a ticking time bomb.

I liken access control to self-respect and boundaries in my life. I had always loved nondiscretionary posts because it meant no one could get through that access point except the protectee and Secret Service. There was a concrete answer to anyone else attempting to gain access. No. It angered some people, especially those who thought they were entitled to access.

In my hurt and sadness after divorce and unemployment, I turned into a nondiscretionary post. I simply didn't allow anyone to get close enough to hurt me again. When I briefly allowed someone in after Steve and I had split, I got hurt, and that reinforced my assumption of safety in isolation. A nondiscretionary post turns into a lonely place in a hurry though, and my isolation was anything but healthy.

Effective access control goes beyond merely keeping the wrong people out. It's also about knowing when to revoke access for the sake of my well-being. My circle of friends got a lot smaller after I left the Secret Service. Unfortunately, part of self-respect meant acknowledging one-sided friendships were hurting my ability to move in a positive direction. I had to start standing up for myself, and that wasn't received well by one longtime friend from childhood. I was called selfish, and she's the only person who has ever called me that, at least to my face.

I thought something was wrong with me. My friendships and relationships didn't work because I wasn't good enough or giving enough. I thought no one would want to be around the new me who was trying to implement an effective yet welcoming security plan in her life. I sometimes wondered if I was too impulsive to revoke access to people I'd known for so long, second-guessing my intuition because I didn't want to be selfish.

I'm grateful to the people who popped into my life during this time, people who showed me kindness when I was in my nondiscretionary post days.

I met a lady via a pet-sitting website, who watched my dogs for the first time when I went to Miami Beach. She asked me to go hiking with her one day a few months later. She didn't know that particular day was an exceptionally lonely one, and despite wanting to stay in the apartment and sulk, I went with her and had a great time. My apartment managers were two of the kindest people I've ever met. They were always full of encouragement even though they didn't know me well. I took the dogs to the Boneyard, a Culver City dog park, a couple of days each week. A lady there asked me to go hiking near Loyola Marymount University a few times.

When I was ready to isolate myself indefinitely, it seemed like someone would appear in my life to remind me that access control is not about building walls with no doors; it's about being receptive to positive requests for access and selective about who and what influences me.

This concept of access control may seem rudimentary to some people. Too simple. But to my former agent mindset, viewing relationships as access points was my way of gaining self-respect and establishing boundaries after many years of inadequate self-care and self-awareness. I needed to be as assertive in my healing and growth as I was at nondiscretionary posts as an agent.

As I navigated this new access-control mindset, I received some clarity about another topic: modesty and exposure. Sexuality, especially for women, is something expressed in a multitude of ways. Body positivity and body confidence were terms tossed around every time I turned on the television or walked past a magazine rack at Vons. I envied the confidence of women who flaunted their curves and embraced their cellulite and flaws. I loved the energy they were generating among women. Lord knows, I could have used a lot more of this positivity in my own life.

As I've said, I wasn't dating by the time I had moved into my Los Angeles apartment, but it's not because I didn't want to. No one expressed interest except for my neighbor who was the local pot dealer, a former pimp, and older than my dad. I thought maybe I was just too plain for Los Angeles. I knew I wasn't a prude, but I wanted to feel desirable. I still struggled with thinking another human was responsible for making me feel better about myself. Just because I learned something didn't mean implementing it was a piece of cake.

My wardrobe for the previous nine years consisted of mostly business suits and athletic attire. I rarely wore my hair down because I hated when hair would get caught in my earpiece. Plus I didn't want my hair flying in my face if I needed to run or react quickly. I hadn't anticipated the need to build a new wardrobe after the Secret Service, but it definitely brought out the fashionista side of me. It also prompted thoughts about modesty as I tried to figure out what would make me feel sexier.

I lived in a predominately Jewish community, and many abided by the Orthodox modesty standards. I naively assumed that women who wore flowy, long, and nonformfitting clothes lacked body positivity. But as I spoke with the women in my neighborhood, they made me realize the body does not have to be exposed to demonstrate body confidence or body positivity. To most of them, modesty was not about making oneself deliberately unattractive but about privacy and self-respect.

I found their perspective refreshing and clarifying. Society tends to gravitate toward extremes—like a celebrity posting a nude selfie to demonstrate empowerment. I was inspired by the rebels who didn't subscribe to the notion that overexposure demonstrated more body positivity than selective exposure.

The first few months in the apartment were ones of fashion experimentation. I even made some of my own clothes (terribly), but I started to figure out what I liked and what made me feel best. I wore some weird outfits and went through a phase where I loved wearing old hats and big sunglasses. I felt like my great-grandma Pauline, who had quite the eclectic fashion sense with her over-the-top dime-store jewelry, bright colors, and chain belts. She didn't care what other people thought of her clothes, and I tried to emulate her carefree attitude.

I found the three-by-five-inch card with Josh's words in a box of paperwork one night in the apartment, and I smiled at my loopy cursive writing on the purple card, completely uncharacteristic of the masculine and blocky all-caps writing around me. It was a good reminder that I didn't become a Secret Service agent to be one of the girls, and I definitely didn't leave the job to become one of them either.

Access control—all aspects of it, including self-respect and boundaries as they pertain to relationships and exposure—has been my most difficult Secret Service life lesson. It continues to be something I struggle with.

Right alongside self-respect and establishing healthy boundaries lies self-awareness. The same way the motorcade communicates with the agents at the next destination, I needed to communicate with myself honestly. My Situation Report, or SITREP, could not be declared "all clear" when it wasn't. Being diagnosed with depression and dealing with the eating disorder relapse showed me the underlying strength in asking for help because the Secret Service's Employee Assistance Program did not shun my vulnerability. They embraced it, and I was better for it.

Last but not least, I learned about love from Nancy Reagan when I had felt the most unloved. But I couldn't help but feel I was still missing something. I was establishing boundaries, forming my own opinions, acknowledging when I was not all clear, et cetera.

One early morning, probably around three a.m., I lay awake in my bed, the sound of snoring dogs around me. After staring at the spinning ceiling fan for a few minutes, I realized what I was missing: forgiveness.

Forgiveness is tricky. It's a choice, not necessarily a feeling. I chose to forgive Steve that night. I chose to forgive others who had hurt me too. And I reluctantly made the choice to forgive myself. Don't get me wrong. This wasn't some grandiose spiritual revelation that resulted in instant peace and happiness.

Sometimes I had to remind myself that I had forgiven. I'd think, "If I forgive this person, then it's like saying what they did to me was okay." Pride can get in the way of forgiveness.

The next morning, I caught myself before I could feel sad and lonely. *You've already forgiven.* I don't think the reminders meant I hadn't truly forgiven. I think it meant I was human. People say to forgive and forget, but forgetting is impossible. That's why forgiveness is so important. *Maybe if I remind myself of the forgiveness long enough, I won't wake up thinking about the past after a while.* Forgive first, and then make the choice to grow despite the events that led up to it. Easier said than done.

On October 31, 2016, exactly ten years after my TEA exam (the first step in the Secret Service hiring process when I applied), I heard someone on the television ask this question: How do you want to be remembered?

"Heck if I know," I said. But sometime in the middle of the night, I realized I did, in fact, know the answer. I wiggled out of bed, the dogs moaning at me for disturbing their peace, and wrote it down.

"How do you want to be remembered, Melanie Lentz?

I want people to say I was what love looked like.

I want to be remembered as kind, for kindness stems from love.

I want to be remembered as strong, because a strong lover fights for herself, for her loved ones, and those who can't fight for themselves.

I want to be remembered as lovely, because a lovely person transcends the superficial descriptions of sexy, cute, hot, et cetera. A lovely person is beautiful because she loves.

I want to be remembered as modest in the classiest of ways, for a woman who loves herself respects herself enough to learn her true worth which goes beyond measurements, size, and pressures to overexpose.

I want to be remembered as honest, for honesty itself is a reflection of love in its purest form. Honest love is transparent love, and she's not afraid to show it even if fear and rejection have tainted her past. She just honestly loves anyway.

I want to be remembered as motivated and productive, for a motivated and productive woman doesn't bask in the conveniences of idleness but hustles and produces. She can stand on her own because she loves herself enough to take care of herself.

I want to be remembered as a rejuvenator, for no real woman is a drain on those around her. A rejuvenator loves herself enough to know that building others up is fulfilling in and of itself. Breaking others down to feel full is not love. It's selfish, and selfishness has no place in love. Self-love, yes. Selfishness, no.

I want to be remembered as a fighter, for a woman who fights for what is right is a lover. She won't run at the first sign of trouble. She's committed to her life and those in it. She's not afraid to stand and exchange if it means saving something worth fighting for.

I want to be remembered as humble, never too good for anything. Even if she's a real lady, she's never superior. Never entitled. Never afraid to get her hands dirty and pitch in to help others. She's not afraid to get out of her comfort zone because she loves enough to get the job done.

I want to be remembered because I loved so very hard."

CHAPTER 25

CASE CONTINUED

IN THE SECRET SERVICE, ADMINISTRATIVE paperwork is emphasized… a lot. Paperwork and reports are not fun, but they're a necessary evil. My very first case in the Los Angeles Field Office was a hand-me-down fraud case from another agent.

The Secret Service investigative reports are structured with specific language and formatting. Each report started by referencing the previous investigative reports. In my new case, I needed to reference the previous report written by the previous case agent. My initial draft read something like this:

"Reverence is made to Special Agent (SA) Adam [Last Name]'s previous report continuing this case pending further investigation."

I sent the report to Adam and asked him to take a look since it was originally his case and it was my first report. He called me a couple of hours later, and he was laughing.

"Lentz, I'm so glad you hold my previous reports in such high regard."

"What do you mean?" I asked.

"Well, look at your draft."

"Okay. I'm pulling it up now." I clicked the file open on my desktop.

"Look at your first sentence."

And then I saw it.

"I love being revered," he said, his smirk practically coming through the phone at me.

I wrote *Reverence* instead of *Reference.* Neither my eyes nor spell check caught this little blunder. I'd managed to screw up the first word in my very first report.

Writing my story so far has felt a lot like referencing previous case reports. I don't *revere* my story. But I'm choosing to *reference* the past because it's not going to change. I don't want to repeat the mistakes. With that reference has come reluctant acceptance.

I wish I could say my story wraps up in a little bow, complete with a fairy-tale ending, but I would be lying. I wanted to write a compilation of entertaining Secret Service stories. I've had plenty of interesting experiences in my career, but not all of them convey what's truly meaningful. I wish I could say leaving the Secret Service resulted in immediate happiness and growth, but it didn't.

Those pesky investigative case reports always ended with a final status update. If a case was already prosecuted or in the judicial process, the current case report would end with something like this:

"Case continued pending further judicial action."

If a case was still in the investigative phase, it would say "Case continued pending further investigation."

If a case were being closed altogether, it would simply say "Case closed."

Either way, that final statement was a status update. I don't know what's next for me, but my case isn't closed.

Life is guaranteed to savagely insert plot twists whether I like it or not. It's guaranteed I will be unready for most of them. But despite my flaws and circumstances, I don't want to lose the innocence I started my career with. Innocence, by definition, refers to "lack of guile or corruption; purity." I don't have to be corrupted by the past. Life experience led to wisdom I didn't have before, but it didn't have to rob me of innocence entirely.

Today I love something about myself. I love that my heart has found a more authentic loving place, and I am going in a better direction than I ever was before.

As C. S. Lewis said, "You can't go back and change the beginning, but you can start where you are and change the ending."

Reference (not reverence) is made to all my previous mistakes and successes.

Case continued pending further growth and learning.

AFTERWORD

'VE CONTINUED TO GROW AND struggle. By mid-2017, I sold even more of my already sparse possessions, including my car. I packed what was left in one large shipping box and filled a rental car with the rest. I drove twenty-six hours with the dogs to the Midwest where my parents and most of my extended family had moved. California had been the only place I'd ever called home. I didn't want to live anywhere else.

I knocked on my parents' door with a very humble, "They say when you hit rock bottom, the best thing to do is to go where you last felt home." Unlike Steve, the Secret Service, and others in my life, my family never abandoned me or tossed me aside. I pushed my family away in an effort to prove to myself that I didn't need anybody, to prove that my greatest fear—being alone—was one I could conquer. My family stayed and loved me anyway.

I hope my stories are ultimately an empowering encouragement. I hope it prompts others to reevaluate aspects of their lives that might need a change. I've disclosed a lot about myself in these pages, much of which my coworkers never knew. I was living this put-together lie because the truth wasn't always pretty. Pride comes before the fall, and I suppose I'm no exception.

I loved my job. I was a good US Secret Service special agent, but I'm grateful I recognized and took action when it was time to leave.

I knew I was healing when I could write and talk about the past without wishing I could change it. It was a peaceful day when I was working on this book and thought, *I don't want to go back there.*

Thank you for referencing my "case" with me.

ACKNOWLEDGMENTS

Writing *Agent Innocent* was one of the more difficult challenges I've faced to date, but it was also one of the most healing processes. None of it would have been possible without this long list of wonderful and caring people.

First, I'd like to thank my family, especially my parents, Joe and Sandy. At no point in my life have I ever doubted your love for me. Despite everything, you've been my biggest fan, even when I wasn't my best self and even when I drove to Iowa from California in a rental car because I didn't know what else to do. From swim meets to graduations to meltdowns and beyond, you're the most present parents a lady could ask for. I love you oodles.

To Traci, my sister. You've known me longer than any friend I've made along the way. You've seen me at my best and worst and loved me anyway. Your realism often puts me back on the straight and narrow. Your humor and wit make me smile even on those really bad days. Your huge and generous heart is a blessing in my life. Oh, and thank you for having my adorable nephew, Alex. I just love that kid. And I love you, punk.

To the rest of my extended family, I hope you know how

much your encouragement and support for me has kept me going, especially in the past couple years. Living close by has allowed me to see more of you in two years than I had in the ten before it. I'd truly been missing out. I love you, and I'm grateful for you.

I have always wanted to write, and my friend Carol Sikes helped ignite that fire in high school. Carol, thank you for all those mornings we sat and chatted about characters and scenes for our future projects.

My writing took a long hiatus when I joined the Secret Service, so I must credit Laurie Wagner for reigniting that flame many years later. Thank you for teaching me to "wild write" and for your (sometimes) brutal honesty with the rubbish I produced in your classes. And thank you for referring me to Maya Stein and Lisa Fugard.

Maya Stein, thank you for teaching me the importance of word choice and how fun the selection can be.

Lisa Fugard, my writing mentor, thank you doesn't even come close to being enough. You saw those first crappy drafts and the messy woman behind the keyboard and stuck with me anyway. Your patience and thoughtfulness throughout this process made me a better writer. You helped me find my voice, and that is priceless. I know we both wished the publication timeline and methods were different, but maybe this is for the best. I can't wait to work on the novels with you! Let's get on that ASAP!

Windy Lynn Harris, you and Lisa showed me the art of the personal essay, and I got published for the first time after your Essay Boot Camp. Your attention to detail and incredible knowledge of this crazy industry helped me not only know what I was getting into but also navigate it.

Tracey Jarvis Graves, thank you for your insight and encouragement as I made the difficult choice to self-publish and for pointing me to Anne Victory.

Laura Harrison and the team at Bradley Communications, thank you for all of the help and insight when it comes to marketing myself. Thank you for your patience as I worked on "getting out there."

Anne Victory, Annie Sarac, and the team at Victory Editing, you're wonderful! Thank you for all the painstaking proofreading and tedious formatting. It was a pleasure working with you, and I hope we can do it again soon.

Sue Ann Baker, thank you for writing the foreword for this book and for your friendship. I have enjoyed getting to know you and cherish all of those emails and calls we've exchanged about the book and life in general.

Tim McCarthy, thank you for your service and sacrifice. Thank you also for your encouragement and insight as I was drafting this book. It was a pleasure meeting you at Mrs. Reagan's funeral.

Brit and Adisa, you showed me what real friendship looks like. As fellow lady agents, we navigated a lot and balanced (or attempted to balance) a lot of life with each other. I miss our LAFO coffee and running dates. I miss a lot about the job, but I miss working with you every day the most, besties.

To the agents from SATC 273, LAFO, RPD, and beyond, thank you for the adventures. SATC 273, thank you for looking out for the twenty-two-year-old who didn't have a clue. LAFO, thank you for the roller coaster of adventure, travel, and life lessons. To the agents on RPD, you were an unexpected blessing during the most difficult time in my life. I thought God had forgotten about me, but being surrounded by agents with sound advice and positive attitudes was the best place I could have been considering what was going on outside of work. I am forever grateful. Thank you to the good bosses (Jeremy and Smitty especially) and even the not-so-great ones. Regardless of your supervisory skills, I learned a lot. To the agents still on the job, I see you in the background, and I know you're sacrificing a lot to fulfill the agency's mission. Thank you to all those who remain.

Thank you to my Veritas Connection Group for so lovingly welcoming me into your circle. It's no understatement to say this group has changed my life for the better. Thank you to my OTF Cedar Rapids family and the ladies from my book club. Being the "new kid in town" was not fun, but all those drastic life changes were worth it because I met you. Sometimes things just work out when I least expected.

God, thank You for all of the above and more. It took me a long time to see You working in the background, and so much still doesn't make sense. Thank You for not abandoning me when I was abandoning You. Thank You for my guardian angel, Anja, on July 31, 2016.

MEET MELANIE LENTZ

Website: www.melanielentz.com

Media Inquiries: media@melanielentz.com

General Inquiries: mel@melanielentz.com

Social Media: @melanielentzauthor (Instagram)

@melanielentzofficial (Facebook)

@melanielentz (Twitter)

Made in the USA
San Bernardino, CA
29 November 2019